THE HONEST BROKER

Scientists seeking to play a positive role in policy and politics and contribute to the sustainability of the scientific enterprise have choices in what role they play. This book is about understanding these choices, what considerations are important to think about when deciding, and the consequences of such choices for the individual scientist and the broader scientific enterprise. Rather than prescribing what course of action each scientist ought to take, the book aims to identify a range of options for individual scientists to consider in making their own judgments about how they would like to position themselves in relation to policy and politics. Using examples from a range of scientific controversies and thought-provoking analogies from other walks of life, *The Honest Broker* challenges us all – scientists, politicians, and citizens – to think carefully about how best science can contribute to policy-making and a healthy democracy.

Roger A. Pielke, Jr. is Professor in the Environmental Studies Program and Fellow of the Cooperative Institute for Research in Environmental Sciences (CIRES), University of Colorado at Boulder. In 2006 he was awarded the Eduard Brückner Prize for outstanding achievement in interdisciplinary climate research.

The Honest Broker

MAKING SENSE OF SCIENCE IN POLICY AND POLITICS

Roger A. Pielke, Jr.

 CAMBRIDGE UNIVERSITY PRESS

CAMBRIDGE UNIVERSITY PRESS
Cambridge, New York, Melbourne, Madrid, Cape Town, Singapore, São Paulo, Delhi

Cambridge University Press
The Edinburgh Building, Cambridge CB2 8RU, UK

Published in the United States of America by Cambridge University Press, New York

www.cambridge.org
Information on this title: www.cambridge.org/9780521694810

First published 2007
Fourth printing 2009

Printed in the United Kingdom at the University Press, Cambridge

A catalogue record for this publication is available from the British Library

ISBN 978-0-521-87320-8 hardback
ISBN 978-0-521-69481-0 paperback

The role of the scientist is not to determine which risks are worth taking, or deciding what choices we should take, but the scientist must be involved in indicating what the possible choices, constraints and possibilities are . . . The role of the scientist is not to decide between the possibilities but to determine what the possibilities are.

Lord May, 1990

Contents

Figures

Tables

Acknowledgments

I have been extremely fortunate to have learned from and benefited from collaborations with many wonderful and brilliant people. Many have shaped this manuscript in direct and indirect ways. While I can't acknowledge all of them, I'd like to acknowledge in particular Dan Sarewitz, Rad Byerly, Bobbie Klein, Rich Conant, Genevieve Maricle, Elizabeth McNie, Adam Briggle, Shep Ryen, Nat Logar, Marilyn Averill, Jimmy Hague, Erik Fisher, Roger Pielke, Sr., Susan Avery, Carl Mitcham, Bob Frodeman, Gianfranco Bagone, Lisa Dilling, and Hans von Storch. Ami Nacu-Schmidt's contributions have been, as always, consistently expert and absolutely essential.

The ideas expressed in this book have been sharpened considerably over the past five years by the questions and challenges posed by students in my graduate seminars "Science, Policy, and the Environment" and "Science and Technology Policy" at the University of Colorado. In addition, many of the ideas presented here were incubated in discussions on our weblog, Prometheus. Thanks go to many of the participants in discussion there whose challenges, recommendations, and critiques have proven to be a tremendous intellectual asset.

I would like to give special thanks to the Sigma-Tau Fondazione in Rome, and especially Pino Dongi, for an opportunity to present an early version of the ideas in this book to an Italian audience through their series Lezioni Italiane – as a book *Scienza e politica: La lotta per il consenso* (Rome: Laterza, 2005) and as a series of lectures at the University of Milan in the fall of 2005. Chris Harrison at Cambridge has provided consistently valuable guidance and advice. If I have accomplished only part of what he has envisioned, it will be far better than what I could ever have done on my own. Of course, the standard disclaimer applies: any errors, muddled thinking, or unclear expression in this volume are the sole responsibility of the author.

Chapter 4 draws on material first published in Pielke (2004a), and Chapter 8 draws on an analysis first presented in Pielke (2004b).

Last to acknowledge, but first in all other respects, is my wonderful family, Julie, Megan, Jacob, and Calvin.

ONE

Four idealized roles of science in policy and politics

Imagine that a visitor has come to town to see you, and wants to find some place in town to eat dinner. Being a local, you have expertise that may be useful in helping the visitor make a decision about where to dine. How might you provide information relevant to the decision on where to eat?

This chapter uses this story, with you as the central character, to illustrate four different ways in which you might interact with your guest. These four modes of interaction are very much ideal types; the real world rarely conforms to such distinctions. But the four different roles in fact do reflect practical differences in how scientists (and other experts) relate to policy and politics. Behavior by scientists providing counsel to decision-makers does necessarily approximate one ideal type more or less than another. Thus, these four different roles, while idealized, do reflect that scientists face practically meaningful choices in how they act in the context of policy and politics.

One choice that you might make in providing advice to your visitor is to serve as a *Pure Scientist*. You may decide that you really have no interest in the visitor's decision-making process and simply want to share some fundamental information about factors involved with nutrition. So you might provide your guest with a copy of the

US government's official report, *Dietary Guidelines for Americans*, which describes the characteristics of a healthy diet. What the visitor does with that information you feel is his or her responsibility.

A second role that you might decide to play is that of the *Science Arbiter* who serves as a resource for the visitor, much like a hotel concierge. The visitor could ask you a question, such as "How far is it to the closest Thai restaurants?" or "Where can I find a steakhouse with the lowest prices?" The Science Arbiter serves as a resource for the decision-maker, standing ready to answer factual questions that the decision-maker thinks are relevant. The Science Arbiter does not tell the decision-maker what he or she ought to prefer.

A third role is that of the *Issue Advocate*. That is, you might try to convince the visitor to eat at a particular restaurant. There are many reasons why you might try to limit the visitor's scope of choice, e.g., perhaps you think that the restaurant is really good, or perhaps you think that you understand the visitor's interests well enough to act in his or her stead, or perhaps your cousin works at the restaurant. Such issue advocacy could be very strong if you are focused on advocating a single restaurant, or more relaxed, if you were directing the visitor to some limited set of restaurants, say those with Italian food. The Issue Advocate does venture into telling the visitor what he or she ought to prefer by making the case for one alternative over others.

A fourth and final role is the *Honest Broker of Policy Alternatives* who provides the visitor with information on all restaurants in the city, basic information on each (cost, menu, location, etc.) and then lets the visitor face the challenge of reducing the scope of choice (i.e., making a decision). Such "honest brokering" could also be comprehensive (e.g., a comprehensive guide to all restaurants in the city) or more limited (e.g., a guide to all those within a five-minute walk). The defining characteristic of the honest broker of policy alternatives is an effort to expand (or at least clarify) the scope of choice for decision-making in a way that allows for the decision-maker to reduce choice based on his or her own preferences and values. Because honest brokering of policy alternatives is often best achieved through a collection of experts working together with a range of views, experiences, and knowledge, a good example for restaurants might be a travel guide, such as those published by Fodors or Lonely Planet.

A characteristic fundamental to both Honest Brokers of Policy Alternatives and Issue Advocates is an explicit engagement of decision alternatives (i.e., choices, policy options, forks in the road, etc.). In contrast, the Pure Scientist and Science Arbiter are not concerned with a specific decision, but instead serve as information resources. Ostensibly, the Pure Scientist and Science Arbiter do not seek to compel a particular decision outcome, but in practice often slip into "stealth issue advocacy." The Issue Advocate seeks to compel a particular decision, while an Honest Broker of Policy Alternatives seeks to enable the freedom of choice by a decision-maker. It should also be obvious that as an expert one cannot simultaneously act as an Issue Advocate and an Honest Broker of Policy Alternatives at exactly the same time.[1] That is to say, one cannot work to both reduce and expand choice at the same time. As ideal types these categories are obviously not black and white, but a continuum from strictly reducing choice to expansively presenting options.

Let's follow the analogy a bit further to illustrate some of the complexities involved in trying to serve as a Pure Scientist or Science Arbiter in the context of decision-making. Let's say that you wish to serve as a Pure Scientist in your interactions with the visitor looking for a restaurant, and so you decide to hand the visitor the US government's report on nutrition. In the United States the federal government has come up with something called the "food guide pyramid" which seeks to provide guidelines on what constitutes a healthy diet. The pyramid does not purport to tell you what restaurant to eat at, only the scientific basis for what constitutes a healthy diet (USDA National Agricultural Library 2006). At first consideration, the food guide pyramid might seem to offer the prospects of providing objective science to inform decision-making that is separate from the process of actually making a decision about where to eat. But things are just not so simple, for two reasons.

First, it turns out that the food guide pyramid is reflective of political debates that manifest themselves within the food science community. In other words, rather than representing pure science, the food pyramid actually serves to support issue advocacy. Marion Nestle (2002), who is Professor and Chair of the Department of Nutrition and Food Studies at New York University, has written a book called *Food Politics* that documents the battle of interests that takes place through the guise of food science (e.g., the interests of different food companies, the interests of the food industry as a whole). Professor Nestle served on the federal committee that developed the food guide pyramid and commented in the *Los Angeles Times* that, "Creating the [food pyramid] guidelines is still political – from start to finish. It's science politics. It's politics politics. It's corporate politics" (Mestel 2004). The food guide pyramid does not tell you exactly where to eat, but for those who look to the pyramid to inform their decisions, the food guide pyramid suggests that some choices are more desirable and others less so. Because the guidelines reflect a political process, the pyramid has great potential to serve as a front for "stealth issue advocacy."[2] This is why battles over science take on such importance across a wide range of areas. People can debate policy options through science without ever making their value commitments explicit. They can hide them behind science.

No one should be surprised by this, as scholars have demonstrated in great depth the degree to which considerations of politics and values shape the work of experts seeking to provide guidance to decision-makers. As Sheila Jasanoff, a leading scholar of science and society, has written:

> Although pleas for maintaining a strict separation between science and politics continue to run like a leitmotif through the policy literature, the artificiality of this position can no longer be doubted. Studies

of scientific advising leave in tatters the notion that it is possible, in practice, to restrict the advisory practice to technical issues or that the subjective values of scientists are irrelevant to decision-making . . .

The notion that scientific advisors can or do limit themselves to addressing purely scientific issues, in particular, seems fundamentally misconceived . . . the advisory process seems increasingly important as a locus for negotiating scientific differences that have political weight. (Jasanoff 1990: 249)

But in spite of such findings, a powerful current runs through the scientific enterprise that suggests that science somehow should be kept separate from considerations of policy and politics, even as science is asked to be relevant to decision-making. Policy makers looking to use science to advance their own agendas often reinforce the possibility of a separation between science and politics. The notion of science being at once apart from but a part of politics and policy presents a paradox that will be taken up in some detail later in the book.

A second complexity arises when we realize that there are alternative food pyramids available, such as the "vegetarian food pyramid" (VegSource 2006a), the "vegan food pyramid" (VegSource 2006b), and the "Atkins food pyramid" (Everything Atkins 2002), among many others. The degree to which one of these is "better" than another depends upon the criteria one employs to evaluate them. If one values not eating meat, then the vegetarian food pyramid may be favored over the US government food pyramid. Alternatively, one's food pyramid preference will be influenced if one values the advertised waist-slimming effects of the Atkins diet over concerns about its health effects. The point here is that the expertise relevant to a particular decision – where to eat dinner – will necessarily be a function of what the decision-maker actually values. Absent knowing such values, any food pyramid will reflect either the values of those putting the pyramid together, or the experts' interpretation/expectation of what decision-makers ought to value. Consequently, it is very easy for the food science expert to act as an

Issue Advocate (e.g., should meat be part of the pyramid?) rather than as a Pure Scientist, favoring one set of choices over others based on trans-scientific considerations. In the end, no food pyramid alone can tell the hungry traveler where to eat.

So are there any circumstances in which experts can provide "objective" guidance that is independent of the choices to be made? The answer is yes and no. Perhaps ironically, objectivity is more possible in cases where the decision context is highly specified or constrained. If you have narrowed down your restaurant choices to, say, three restaurants, then you could ask your Science Arbiter to comment on the cost or healthiness of each, according to criteria that you would like to see applied. In circumstances where the scope of choice is fixed and the decision-maker has a clearly defined technical question, then the expert has a very important role to play in serving as an arbiter of science, focused on specific *positive* questions. But in situations where the scope of choice is open, decision-makers do not have a consensus on the values to be served by the decision, much less a fix on the technical questions derived from value commitments. There is very little room for arbitrating science in the process of decision-making and even good faith efforts to provide such a perspective can easily turn into a political battleground where political debate is couched in the guise of a debate over science (and the expert may not even be aware of his/her arguing politics through science).[3]

Daniel Sarewitz, one of the most thoughtful observers of science in society, characterizes the resulting circumstances:

> In areas as diverse as climate change, nuclear waste disposal, endangered species and biodiversity, forest management, air and water pollution, and agricultural biotechnology, the growth of considerable bodies of scientific knowledge, created especially to resolve political dispute and enable effective decision-making, has often been accompanied instead by growing political controversy and gridlock. Science typically lies at the center of the debate, where those who advocate some line of action are likely to claim a scientific justification for their position, while those opposing the action will either

invoke scientific uncertainty or competing scientific results to support their opposition ... nature itself – the reality out there – is sufficiently rich and complex to support a science enterprise of enormous methodological, disciplinary, and institutional diversity. I will argue that science, in doing its job well, presents this richness, through a proliferation of facts assembled via a variety of disciplinary lenses, in ways that can legitimately support, and are causally indistinguishable from, a range of competing, value-based political positions. (Sarewitz 2004: 386)

So when a scientist claims to focus "only on the science," in many cases the scientist risks serving instead as a Stealth Issue Advocate. For some scientists stealth issue advocacy is politically desirable because it allows for a simultaneous claim of being above the fray, invoking the historical authority of science, while working to restrict the scope of choice. The Stealth Issue Advocate seeks to "swim without getting wet."[4] Other scientists may be wholly unaware of how their attempts to focus only on science contribute to a conflation of scientific and political debates. One way for scientists to avoid such conflation, argued throughout this book, is to openly associate science with possible courses of action – that is, to serve as Honest Brokers of Policy Alternatives.[5]

For scientists seeking to play a positive role in policy and politics and contribute to the sustainability of the scientific enterprise there is good news – scientists have choices in what roles they play. *Pure Scientist, Science Arbiter, Issue Advocate,* or *Honest Broker of Policy Alternatives?* All four roles are critically important and necessary in a functioning democracy. But scientists do have to choose. Whether a scientist admits, accepts, or is aware of it, a choice must be made on how he or she relates to the decision-making process. This book is about understanding this choice, what considerations may be important to think about when deciding, and the consequences of such choices for the individual scientist and the broader scientific enterprise.

TWO

The big picture, science, and democracy

Our time is characterized by new demands upon scientists in policy and politics. But experience and research show us that science is well suited to contribute directly to the resolution of political conflicts only in the most simple of decision contexts. In more complicated contexts, looking to science to enable a political consensus may in fact compromise both the odds for consensus and the valuable role that science can provide to policy-making. In the light of these findings, which some scientists may admittedly find uncomfortable, this book considers options available for scientists in policy and politics.

The arguments presented in this book have benefited from, and indeed are derived from, a large literature on Science, Technology, and Society (STS) and Science and Technology Policy (STP).[1] For many scholars of STS or STP the arguments presented in this book may be quite familiar, even old news. But my experiences over the past decade and a half working on a day-to-day basis with many scientists suggest that, with some notable exceptions, most scientists, including social scientists, are simply unaware of the understandings of the scholarly community who study science in society. Hence, it is appropriate to view this work as an attempt to connect scholarly understandings of science in society with the practical world of scientists who increasingly face everyday decisions about how to position their careers and research in the context of policy and politics. Rather than prescribing what course of action each individual scientist ought to take, the aim here is to identify a range of options for individual scientists to consider in making their own judgments on how they would like to position themselves in relation to policy and politics.

Even with a commitment to present a perspective on the scope of choice available to scientists in policy and politics, a central argument throughout this book is that as science has become used increasingly as a tool of *politics*, its role in *policy* has arguably been overshadowed. To use the concepts introduced in Chapter 1, the scientific enterprise has a notable shortage of Honest Brokers of Policy Alternatives, with many scientists instead choosing to engage policy and politics as Issue Advocates, or more troubling for the sustainability of the scientific enterprise, as Stealth Issue Advocates. Honest Brokers of Policy Alternatives matter because a powerful role for science in society is to facilitate the creation of new and innovative policy alternatives. Such alternatives have the potential to reshape political dynamics and, in some cases, enable action. By understanding the different roles that science plays in both policy and politics we may enhance the benefits to society related to the public's substantial investments in generating new knowledge.

Without a doubt science has demonstrated its enormous value to society and continues to have great potential to contribute significantly to further improving societal and environmental conditions. However, for that potential to be more fully realized, we must adopt a perspective on science that allows room for a close engagement with policy. If scientists ever had the choice to remain above the fray, they no longer have this luxury. It has become widely accepted by the public and policy-makers (and most scientists as well) that science shows relevance to a wide range of societal problems. Consequently, we should not view science as an activity to be kept separate from policy and politics but, instead, as a key resource for facilitating complicated decisions that involve competing interests in society. We want science to be connected to society. But how we make this connection is not always easy or obvious. This book seeks to provide some conceptual clarity about the choices scientists face in connecting their work to policy and politics. The choices matter, not just for science and science in policy, but more broadly for how we think about the role of expertise in democracy.

Chapter 1 argued that scientists, and other experts have choices in how they relate their work to policy and politics. Understanding such choices is important if science is to contribute to common interests. Science in the service of common interests is threatened as scientists and policy-makers have come to see science mainly as a servant of interest group politics. That is to say, increasingly, science has come to be viewed as simply a resource for enhancing the ability of groups in society to bargain, negotiate, and compromise in pursuit of their special interests. As a consequence, groups with otherwise conflicting interests each look to science to enhance their political standing. The result is that political battles are played out in the language of science, often resulting in policy gridlock and the diminishment of science as a resource for policy-making.

Two Congressional hearings in the summer of 2006 dramatically illustrated these dynamics. The hearings were putatively about studies of the global temperature record over the past several thousand years and efforts to clarify scientific understandings about this history. In reality the hearings were about something else altogether, as described by a member of Congress to a scientific witness who had chaired a report suggesting that earlier studies of the paleo-climate record had some flaws and limitations.[2]

> I want you to make sure you understand the reality of this situation. I've given you all the sincerity that I could give to you. But the reason you are here is not why you think you are here, OK? The reason you are here is to try to win a debate with some industries in this country

who are afraid to look forward to a new energy future for this nation. And the reason you are here is to try to create doubt about whether this country should move forward with the new technological, clean-energy future, or whether we should remain addicted to fossil fuels. That's the reason you are here.

The member of Congress was telling the scientist that whether he knew it or not, the hearing was about energy policy actions related to climate change, irrespective of the scientific content being discussed. The scientist was being used as a Stealth Issue Advocate, either knowingly or unknowingly. Another member of Congress at the hearing suggested that given the reality of stealth issue advocacy scientists should consider self-censoring their views based on how they might be received in the political arena. Another scientist present criticized this perspective, suggesting that once scientists start tailoring their scientific results to suit the needs of politics that is when science ceases to be science and morphs completely into politics, threatening the sustainability of the scientific enterprise itself.

Must scientists be at the mercy of politics? The answer is "no," but empowerment depends on understanding the different options available for relating to policy and politics.

Our thinking about the role of experts in democracy is no doubt grounded in how we conceive of the notion of democracy itself. Consequently, how each of us thinks about the Pure Scientist, Science Arbiter, Issue Advocate, and Honest Broker of Policy Alternatives is likely related to our beliefs about two relationships: (a) the role of science in society, and (b) the role of the expert in a democracy.

One well-understood conception of how democracy serves common interests is that competing factions engage one another in political debate, and the resulting compromise reflects the best possible balancing of conflicting demands. Political scientists have called this notion of democracy "interest group pluralism" and it is well described in the writings of James Madison (1787), for example, as is found in *Federalist 10*, which Madison wrote when arguing for adoption of the original US Constitution in the late eighteenth century. Under such a view of Madisonian democracy, experts would best serve society simply by aligning themselves with their favored faction or interest group, and offering their special expertise as an asset in political battle. From this perspective on the role of experts in a democracy, it is a virtue for scientists to take a more proactive role as advocates in political debates seeking to use their authority and expertise as resources in political battles.

An objection to such a conception of democracy, and the role of experts it implies, was offered by political scientist E. E. Schattschneider in his book *The Semi-Sovereign People* (1975). Schattschneider argued that democracy is a competitive system in which the public is allowed to participate by voicing its views on alternatives presented to it in the political process. Such alternatives do not come up from the grassroots any more than you or me telling an auto mechanic what the options are for fixing a broken car. Policy alternatives come from experts. It is the role of experts in such a system to clarify the implications of their knowledge for action and to provide such implications in the form of policy alternatives to decision-makers who can then decide among different possible courses of action.

These different perspectives on democracy are complemented by different views of the role of science in society. In the post-World War II era the United States adopted a perspective on science that scholars have called the "linear model." The linear model takes two forms, one as a general model for how to make decisions about science, emphasizing the importance of basic research. The linear model will be familiar to most in terms of a metaphor that represents a flow of knowledge from basic research to applied research to development and ultimately societal benefits. Since World War II, the linear model has been used to advocate policies for science that emphasize the importance of basic research and freedom for scientists from political accountability.

A second form of the linear model is as specific guidance for the role of science in the context of specific decisions. Specifically, the linear model is often used to suggest that achieving agreement on scientific knowledge is a prerequisite for a political consensus to be reached and then policy action to occur. For instance, this perspective is reflected on the website of the US Environmental Protection Agency in its description of the role of science in the agency: "Through research that is designed to reduce uncertainties, our understanding increases and, as a result, we change our assumptions about the impacts of environmental problems and how they should be addressed" (EPA 2006). In even stronger forms, some use the linear model to argue that specific knowledge or facts compel certain policy responses on topics as varied as the availability of genetically modified foods and over-the-counter emergency contraception.

Arguments that a particular fact or body of knowledge compels a particular decision have been generally critiqued in terms of what is called the "is–ought problem" first raised by philosopher David Hume, who argued simply that you can't get an "ought" (i.e., something which should be done, or an answer to a "normative" question) from an "is" (i.e., a statement of fact, or an answer to a "positive" question).[3] Even so, claims that facts compel certain actions are frequently found in political debates involving scientific issues.

The linear model in both of its forms has been challenged by a range of scholars who have characterized it as descriptively inaccurate and normatively undesirable. Science policy scholar Harvey Brooks offers an alternative view to the linear model in terms of a complex pattern of feedbacks between researchers and decision-makers:

> If the process of using science for social purposes is thought of as one of optimally matching scientific opportunity with social need, then the total evaluation process must embody both aspects in an appropriate mix. Experts are generally best qualified to assess the opportunity for scientific progress, while broadly representative laymen in

TABLE 2.1: *Four idealized roles for scientists in decision-making*

		View of science	
		Linear model	Stakeholder model
View of democracy	Madison	Pure Scientist	Issue Advocate
	Schattschneider	Science Arbiter	Honest Broker of Policy Alternative

close consultation with experts may be best qualified to assess societal need. The optimal balance between opportunity and need can only be arrived at through a highly interactive, mutual education process involving both dimensions. (Brooks 1995: 33)

Similar alternatives to the linear model have been offered by Donald Stokes in the notion of "use-inspired basic research" and Philip Kitcher with "well-ordered science" (also, cf., Jasanoff 1990; Nowotny *et al.* 2001; Sarewitz 1996; Wynne *et al.* 2005). Each of these perspectives suggests some form of "stakeholder model" as an alternative to the linear model of the relationship of science and decision-making. A stakeholder model holds not only that the users of science should have some role in its production but that considerations of how science is used in decision-making are an important aspect of understanding the effectiveness of science in decision-making.

Combinations of these different conceptions of democracy and science provide a simple and straightforward theoretical basis for the four idealized roles for scientists (and experts more generally) in decision-making introduced in Chapter 1, as illustrated in Table 2.1.

Pure scientist (Madisonian democracy + linear model of science)

The Pure Scientist focuses on research with absolutely no consideration for its use or utility, and thus in its purest form has no direct connection with decision-makers. Research results in findings that are placed into a reservoir of knowledge where they will be available to all decision-makers. Those from various factions in society have access to the reservoir from which they can draw the knowledge that they need to clarify and argue their interests. In principle, from this perspective the scientist remains removed from the messiness of policy and politics.

Examples of the Pure Scientist can be found more frequently in myth rather than practice. A young Albert Einstein is often invoked as the canonical pure scientist, seeking only truth without consideration for the practical implications of the results of his research. In practice, of course, things are quite a bit more complicated. Research funding has to be justified, and increasingly this occurs on the basis of expected societal benefits or outcomes. And irrespective of the justifications used in securing support, research results do have implications for the broader society. Even Einstein became active in politics later in his career, warning the United States government of the implications of the development of an atomic bomb.

Issue Advocate (Madisonian democracy + stakeholder model of science)

The Issue Advocate focuses on the implications of research for a particular political agenda. Unlike the Pure Scientist, the Issue Advocate aligns him/herself with a group (a faction) seeking to advance its interests through policy and politics. The Issue Advocate accepts the notion that science must be engaged with decision-makers and seeks to participate in the decision-making process.

Issue Advocates are found everywhere, and science is no exception. Whether the issue is a presidential election, the Nuclear Test Ban Treaty, or the Kyoto Protocol, many scientists are willing to take sides in a contested political issue and use their status as scientists, or invoke their specialized expertise, to argue for their cause. For some scientists advocacy poses difficult questions. For instance, the 2006 meeting of the Society for Conservation Biology held a debate on whether conservation biologists should engage in overt advocacy or instead should strive to stay away from politics and focus only on science (Marris 2006).

Science Arbiter (Schattschneiderian democracy + linear model of science)

The Science Arbiter seeks to stay removed from explicit considerations of policy and politics like the Pure Scientist, but recognizes that decision-makers may have specific questions that require the judgment of experts, so unlike the Pure Scientist the Science Arbiter has direct interactions with decision-makers. The Science Arbiter seeks to focus on issues that can be resolved by science, which may originate in questions raised by decision-makers or debate among decision-makers. In practice, such questions are sent for adjudication to the scientist(s), who may be on an assessment panel or advisory committee, which renders a judgment and returns to the policy-makers scientific results, assessments or findings. A key characteristic of the Science Arbiter is a focus on *positive* questions that can in principle be resolved through scientific inquiry. In principle, the Science Arbiter avoids *normative* questions and thus seeks to remain above the political fray, preferring to inform decision-making through relevant research or assessments, but removed from a closer interaction with stakeholders.[4]

Science Arbiters can take the form of a formal, authoritative committee or organization, such as committees under the National

Research Council or a federal agency. Individual scientists also seek to be Science Arbiters when they seek to answer questions posed by policy-makers or the media. The defining characteristic of the Science Arbiter is a focus on positive scientific questions posed by decision-makers. As will be seen, successfully arbitrating positive scientific questions is replete with incentives to engage in issue advocacy, and thus in practice can be a difficult role to fill.

Honest Broker of Policy Alternatives (Schattschneiderian democracy + stakeholder model of science)

The Honest Broker of Policy Alternatives engages in decision-making by clarifying and, at times, seeking to expand the scope of choice available to decision-makers. Unlike the Science Arbiter, the Honest Broker of Policy Alternatives seeks explicitly to integrate scientific knowledge with stakeholder concerns in the form of alternative possible courses of action.

Like the Science Arbiter, the Honest Broker of Policy Alternatives is likely to take the form of a formal, authoritative committee or assessment. There are several reasons why this is so. First, it can be difficult, and in some cases impossible, for an individual scientist to represent all of the areas of expertise required to recommend a range of action alternatives. Further, a diversity of perspectives can help to militate against issue advocacy (stealth or otherwise). The defining difference between the Issue Advocate and the Honest Broker of Policy Alternatives is that the latter seeks to place scientific understandings in the context of a smorgasbord of policy options. Such options may appeal to a wide range of interests. For example, in the United States the congressional Office of Technology Assessment (which was terminated in the 1990s) often produced reports with a wide set of policy options contingent on ends to be achieved. A simple way to think about the key difference between the Honest Broker of Policy Alternatives and the Issue

Advocate is that the latter seeks to reduce the scope of available choice, while the former seeks to expand (or at least clarify) the scope of choice.

The remainder of this book is focused on developing and understanding several simple criteria that might be fruitfully applied to the question of what role scientists should play in what decision contexts under the goals of contributing productively to effective decision-making and sustaining the long-term viability of the scientific enterprise. I argue that there are two critical factors to consider when a scientist (or any other expert) or scientific organization faces a decision about how to engage with policy and politics. The first criterion is the degree of values consensus on a particular issue. Sharply contested issues raise the political stakes and introduce dynamics quite different from issues which are less controversial. The second criterion is the degree of uncertainty present in a particular decision context. The greater the uncertainty – both scientific and political – the more important it is for science to focus on policy options rather than simply scientific results. The application of the simple criteria developed in the book is illustrated in the flow chart (see Figure 2.1).

Chapter 3 explains why values and uncertainty are central to understanding how science plays different roles in different decision contexts. In short, in the pursuit of desired outcomes, decisions matter and information matters. But in a particular policy context information only very rarely provides a sufficient basis to determine which course of action ought to be taken.

Chapter 4 will discuss the role of values in how we think about the different roles of science in policy and politics. Making things even more complicated is that information will play a different role in decision-making when there is broad agreement on values versus a situation characterized by values conflict. This chapter explains why scholars of science in society have concluded that consideration of values is just as important as issues of science in policy and politics. It uses an extended thought experiment to suggest how scientists

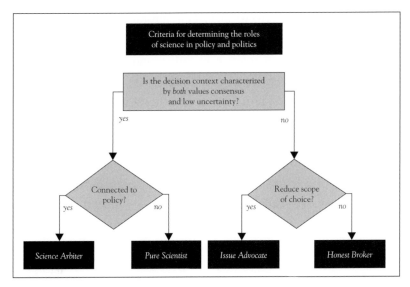

Figure 2.1 Flow chart illustrating the logic of roles for scientists in policy and politics

might determine whether a particular situation is characterized by a broad values consensus or fundamental conflict.

It is easy to conflate scientific uncertainty with political uncertainty, and then to suggest that a reduction in the former compels a reduction in the latter (Chapter 5). Understanding the relationship of different conceptions of uncertainty can help to make sense of different perspectives on the role of science in decision-making. Sometimes scientific research actually increases uncertainty, at least on the time scales of policy-making. This chapter explains different conceptions of uncertainty, how political uncertainty is related to scientific uncertainty, and how scientists might determine whether a particular situation is likely to have scientific or political uncertainty resolved through research.

More broadly, expectations that consensus on science can lead to a consensus in politics have their roots in the "linear model" of the relationship of science and society (Chapter 6). The linear model has been found to be an accurate description of the role of science and decision-making only in special circumstances, where values are shared and uncertainty is low. One of the most significant influences of the linear model on science in policy and politics has been to foster "stealth issue advocacy" among scientists.

Chapters 7 and 8 explore these themes in the context of two cases. Chapter 7 considers policy, politics, and uncertainty in the case of decision-making by the administration of George W. Bush leading to the war in Iraq. Chapter 8 examines the very public debate over the publication of the book *The Skeptical Environmentalist* by Lomborg. In both cases Issue Advocates sought to use science to advance a political agenda. Decision-making arguably suffered in each case because of the lack of Honest Brokers of Policy Alternatives who might have contributed to debate by focusing attention on policy options and their consequences. The concluding chapter (Chapter 9) offers practical recommendations for scientists seeking to better connect their work with decision-makers.

Figure 2.1 illustrates how the various arguments of the book come together to provide a general and simple guide for scientists to assess what roles they might adopt in specific policy and political contexts. For individual scientists or scientists working together, for example, on an advisory committee or assessment, the purpose of this flow chart is to help them make decisions about how to connect their work with decision-makers in ways that are likely to be more effective, that is, to have a better likelihood of helping decision-makers achieve their desired goals while contributing to the long-term sustainability of the scientific enterprise. To use this framework requires that the scientist is to gain some understanding of the broader social and political context of which his or her research is a part.

Beyond individual scientists, there is also a broader perspective. Effective, democratic decision-making depends upon a healthy diversity of roles played by scientists in society. If it is important for the scientific enterprise to advance knowledge and serve stakeholders, and to both serve special interests as well as common interests, then it is important that the scientific community fulfill each of the four roles of scientists in policy and politics. Collective behavior that overlooks one or more of the idealized roles can lead to pathologies in the relationship of science with decision-making.

The flow chart begins by asking whether the context is characterized by a values consensus and low (scientific) uncertainty. Answering yes to both of these questions points toward the Pure Scientist or Science Arbiter as likely being the most effective roles for the scientist, with the final determination between the two assessed by whether or not the scientist has some explicit connection to policy-makers, e.g., such as through a scientific assessment process where explicit questions from decision-makers are used to shape the information reported from the scientific community. Answering no to either of the questions of values or uncertainty points toward the Issue Advocate and Honest Broker of Policy Alternatives, with the final determination between the two decided by whether the scientist seeks to expand (or clarify) or reduce the scope of choice available to decision-makers, with the former associated with the Honest Broker of Policy Alternatives and the latter with the Issue Advocate. This book and the two detailed case studies are focused on exploring this flow chart.

In the end the decision about what role to play by scientists in society will be made by individual scientists, their leaders, and patrons. In the spirit of the theme of this book, it is important to recognize that such decisions can be made in a number of different ways, with important consequences for science, policy, and politics.

THREE

Science and decision-making

This chapter introduces several of the main themes of the book by addressing the following two questions:

- Can science compel action?
- What are "policy," "politics," and "science"?

The answer to the first question is "sometimes," but only in very specific decision contexts characterized by general agreement on valued outcomes and little uncertainty between particular actions and the achievement of outcomes associated with those actions. Such situations are rarely controversial. The answers to the second question are that "policy" is a decision, a commitment to a particular course of action. "Politics" refers to bargaining, negotiation, and compromise in pursuit of desired ends. Understanding these concepts can provide a bit of analytical rigor in defining concepts such as the "politicization of science" and "scientization for policy." Understanding the complex interrelationship of science, policy, and politics is a first step toward making sense of the different roles of scientists who seek to contribute to effective decision-making and sustaining the scientific enterprise.

Can science compel action?

Late at night on July 1, 2002, high over southern Germany two planes streaked across the sky on a collision course. One was a DHL cargo jet and the other a Russian charter carrying students on their way to vacation in Spain. As the planes approached each other, the onboard computerized collision avoidance system on the Russian charter warned the pilot to climb higher. But at just about the same instant over the radio a ground controller told the Russian pilot to dive. The pilot found himself at what philosopher John Dewey called a "forked-road situation," one "which is ambiguous, which presents a dilemma, which proposes alternatives" (Dewey 1997: 11). Afterwards, a newspaper article characterized the situation succinctly, "What lay in the balance was a simple decision: up or down, 1 or 0. Believe the controller or believe the machine" (Johnson 2002).

For the Russian pilot the situation was *uncertain*, meaning that more than one possible outcome was consistent with his under-standing of the choices available to him and their possible conse-quences. The state of uncertainty is a fundamentally human quality because it refers to how we associate our perceptions of the world with our expectations of how we find the world to be. In the absence of perception there is no uncertainty. When our perceptions suggest that only one outcome is possible, there is no uncertainty and we are sure. Of course, we are often very certain and very wrong. Our per-ceptions often mislead us into misjudgments about uncertainty. Misjudgments can lead to poor decisions, sometimes with tragic consequences.

The Russian pilot actually faced three possible choices: dive, climb, or take no action, with each choice leading to two possible outcomes: survive or crash. The pilot's *decision* – his commitment to a particular course of action among his available alternatives – clearly mattered as his choice would shape outcomes in a very profound way. The entire point of making a decision is to reduce uncertainty in a particular, desired direction, or, in other words, to increase the certainty of realizing desired outcomes. From this perspective a *policy* is simply a decision – a commitment to a course of action.[1] In this case, the conflicting information provided by the air traffic controller and onboard computer meant that before making his decision the pilot was unable to use information to reduce uncertainty about the outcomes associated with his options. The information did not compel a certain decision.

The pilot chose to listen to the ground controller and sent the plane into a dive. With hindsight we know that he made the wrong decision, as the planes slammed into each other killing all seventy-one people aboard the two aircraft.

The Russian pilot faced a relatively simple decision situation. Simple decision situations share the following characteristics:

- The scope of choice of is unambiguous, discrete, and bounded.
- No ambiguity exists about the desirability of the different outcomes.
- No ambiguity exists in the relationship between alternative actions and desired outcomes.
- And improving information on which decisions are based promises insight into understanding the relationship of alternative courses of action and desired outcomes.

The Russian pilot's decision-making process was confounded by conflicting information leading to ambiguity between his understanding of available choices and their outcomes. Improving decision-making, and thus outcomes, in such simple decision situations often requires improving the information on which decisions are based, or improving the use of information, often a significant but nonetheless tractable challenge.

Now consider a very different decision situation. For more than a decade, beginning in early 1980s, medical experts advocated mammograms for women age forty and over as a way to screen for early signs of breast cancer (Kolata and Moss 2002). During this period most forty-something women typically did not need to make a conscious decision about being examined because experts routinely recommended mammograms as a way to reduce the risks of breast cancer. But beginning in the early 1990s, health experts began to raise questions about the effectiveness of mammograms. In other words, health experts began to question whether routine mammograms in fact led to desired health outcomes. This increase in uncertainty led the National Cancer Institute, an agency of the US National Institutes of Health (NIH), in 1993 to drop its recommendation of routine screening for forty-year-olds. In 1997 NIH reaffirmed its 1993 decision; however, the US Senate voted to encourage NIH to reverse this guidance, and the nongovernmental American Cancer Society recommended routine screening for all women over forty. In 2001 the debate intensified following the results of a Danish study that questioned the value of all routine mammogram screening, regardless of age. *The Wall Street Journal* reported, "A fierce scientific debate about the true value of mammography screening has left women confused and uncertain about the test" (Parker-Pope 2002).

So what should a woman in her forties do?[2] As with the situation faced by the pilot, her choices are clear. She can opt for routine screening or she can choose not to undergo routine screening. But she must make a decision. Ignoring the issue and going along as she always has done, still leads to a commitment to a particular course of action. Unlike the one-time decision faced by the pilot, a woman continuously faces a decision about mammograms. Deciding to opt out of routine screening today does not mean that a different decision cannot be made tomorrow. A continuous decision process is more complicated than a one-time, discrete choice.

Just like the aircraft on a collision course, a desired outcome related to the mammogram decision is clear and unambiguous: life is preferred over death; health is preferred to illness; efficacious medical tests are preferred to the superfluous. But for at least two reasons in the case of mammograms, the scope of outcomes is not limited only to physical health.

First, mammograms are a tool not only for protecting physical health but also psychological health, and these two outcomes are not necessarily one and the same. One oncologist observed, "People cling to mammograms. They cling to the idea that there is something they can do to protect themselves. If we take away that as a security blanket, people turn to you and say, 'So, what am I supposed to do?'" (Kolata 2002). The psychological factors help to explain why in 1997 the US Senate involved itself in recommending mammograms, even as the science remained uncertain – the senators were seeking to meet the demands of their constituents for guidance on mammograms. For most people, peace of mind is more desirable than anxiety, even if the peace of mind is not backed up by sound data on the effectiveness of the medical procedure.

Second, there are consequences for society related to how millions of women make decisions about mammograms. Routine screening has costs, with implications for health insurance providers, medical practitioners, government budgeting, and electoral politics. When a group of people commit to a particular course of action with broad implications, we call this a *policy*. Often we think of policy as a governmental decision; however, policies are adopted by companies, interest groups, neighborhood associations, school boards, families, individuals and so on. Throughout this book the term *policy* is used to refer to a group's decision – a group's commitment to a particular course of action.

Insurers, doctors, and elected officials each have visions (and typically multiple visions within each community) of desirable outcomes associated with alternative mammogram policies. The visions of these different groups are typically not compatible. For instance, doctors may wish to emphasize health outcomes over costs, insurers may seek a different balance between the two, governments may wish to expand or limit coverage of public heath benefits, and elected officials may want higher approval ratings. The different vested interests of these groups contribute to their provision of various and potentially conflicting advice. As a consequence, an individual woman's decision about whether or not to undergo routine mammograms is shaped by the broader expectations of various groups and institutions in the health care field about the consequences of recommending routine screening.

Like the pilot who received different advice from the computer and the air traffic controller, women receive conflicting guidance on mammograms. A key difference in the case of mammograms is that the outcome associated with an individual decision cannot be immediately known, or perhaps ever known. When a woman chooses to be screened (or not) for mammograms there is more than one possible outcome. According to the 2001 Danish study, women routinely screened for mammograms experienced a death rate no lower than those who went unscreened, yet the screened women experienced more surgical procedures, leading the researchers to ask "whether the test does more harm than good" (Kolata and Moss 2002). And given the context of this uncertainty, it seems unlikely that another study of breast cancer screening will provide clearer understandings of the relationship between alternative courses of action and desired outcomes, at least for women making decisions about mammograms in the near future. One doctor commented on the state of mammogram science, "Uncertainty is very painful. The idea that science is not going to give you certitude is very difficult for many people to accept" (Kolata 2002).

Given the conflicting scientific studies and the long time required for new clinical studies, efforts to improve the information which informs individual and societal decisions about routine screening is unlikely to reduce uncertainty about the relationship of mammogram decisions and health outcomes, at least in the short term. Of course, over the longer term such studies may well be able to clarify the benefits (and costs) of routine mammograms.

At first, uncertainty might appear to stymie effective decision-making, but uncertainty does not mean that women cannot make effective health decisions. By contrast, the uncertainty associated with the effectiveness of mammogram screening could provide an impetus for women in pursuit of physical and psychological health to seek out more choices beyond a "yes or no" decision over mammogram screening. For example, women might focus more upon risk factors for breast cancer and behaviors that might be adopted to reduce those risks. If the goal is health, then women have many options for action that make good sense with respect to their health benefits. Such actions can be considered robust to the presence of uncertainty. As Dwight D. Eisenhower once said, "If a problem cannot be solved, enlarge it" (*The Economist* 2006: 41). Doctors can serve a valuable role in this process as honest brokers of options that women may not be aware of.

The case of mammograms involves some complexities not present in the decision problem faced by the Russian pilot.

- The scope of choice is unambiguous, but it is also continuous.
- For society, conflict exists about the desirability of different outcomes, because there are multiple possible outcomes and multiple conflicting interests.
- Considerable ambiguity exists in the relationship between alternative actions and desired outcomes.
- And improving information promises little insight into the course(s) of action likely to lead to a desired outcome, at least over the near term. But other options are available that might lead to desired outcomes.

With these additional complexities, the case of mammograms provides a hint of the complexities of decision-making in highly politicized contexts involving both science and politics. Such decision contexts are characterized by unbounded alternatives and many possible outcomes associated with those alternatives. The very existence of a problem compelling a decision is often in dispute.

Dewey's "forked-road situation" is itself subject to debate, with some arguing that a particular decision is needed, others arguing that no decision is needed, and still others trying to introduce new forks in the road, leading to various different destinations. These situations are characterized typically not only by lack of consensus on the relationship between alternative courses of action and their outcomes, but lack of consensus on the desirability of particular outcomes.

In all contexts the sole purpose of decision-making is to reduce uncertainty about the future in a preferred direction. That is, by committing to particular courses of action we seek to make some desired outcomes more certain than other, less desirable outcomes. Good decisions are thus those that more reliably lead to desired outcomes. Of course, because in society there are a multitude of interests and perspectives, there is thus rarely (if ever) consensus on desired outcomes and the means to achieve those outcomes. In situations where there is consensus on ends and means, we typically find little conflict. As a result, whenever there is conflict, we engage in political behavior. *Politics* is the process of bargaining, negotiation, and compromise that, in the words of the political scientist Harold Lasswell, determines "who gets what, when, and how" (Lasswell 1958: 96).[3]

When there is conflict over decision-making, politics is necessary to reach a consensus that allows action to occur. So while policy-making thus inevitably has politics, policy and politics are not one and the same. In some systems of governance, politics may involve threats, coercion, injury, and other forms of violence by the powerful upon the weak. In a democracy, or at least a well-functioning democracy, individuals and various interests generally expect to participate in the making of important decisions. The challenge of securing such participation helps to explain why many democratic systems are so complicated and allow for many opportunities to influence the decision-making process.

What are "policy," "politics," and "science"?

The situation faced by the Russian pilot and the women deciding upon a mammogram are both examples of a common problem. We often need information to help guide the making of important decisions, but for various reasons information is rarely sufficient to determining how a decision should be made. And in some cases the wrong information or the misuse of information can actually lead to decisions with undesirable outcomes, and perhaps outcomes that are worse than if the information had not been considered in the first place. More than ever decision-makers depend upon scientific information in the making of important decisions. But at the same time the role of science in decision-making has never been more complicated. For those whose job it is to create, interpret, and provide information to decision-makers, a challenge exists in how to connect their activities with decision-makers in ways that foster good decisions that increase the likelihood of attaining desired outcomes.

In many different contexts, controversies abound about the roles of scientific information in decision-making. In the United States in 2004, Congressman Henry Waxman (D-CA) and the Union of Concerned Scientists, an advocacy group, each issued reports alleging that the administration of George W. Bush systematically misused science in pursuit of its political agenda. And coming from a very different political perspective, the Hoover Institution published a book in 2003 alleging that the political left misuses science to further its political agenda (Gough 2003). Every day when you pick up the paper, watch the news, or surf the internet, science infuses numerous issues of critical importance to health, the environment, the economy, and our security. Consequently, more than ever, making sense of science in policy and politics can help inform both scientists and the users of science about the various roles of science in decision-making.

But if we are to make sense of science in policy and politics we must first start with a shared understanding of what these terms mean in practice. As used in this book, *science* refers to the systematic pursuit of knowledge, and is a broad enough term to share considerable similarities across different areas of knowledge acquisition and expertise, such as, for example, the gathering, interpretation, and dissemination of military intelligence. As described above, *policy* refers to a commitment to a particular course of action, and *politics* refers to the process of bargaining, negotiation, and compromise that determines who gets what, when, and how. Thus, this book is about making sense of the roles played by the systematic pursuit of knowledge for (a) making commitments to particular courses of action and (b) bargaining, negotiation, and compromise, with a particular focus on the role of scientists in policy and politics.

One reason for this focus on scientists is that the role of science in society is changing. Scientists are being asked by policy-makers to contribute more directly to the needs of society. Part of this demand lies in the degree to which the problems that society faces have some close connection to issues of science and technology, for example in areas such as disease, development, terrorism, environmental impacts, adoption of new technologies, and so on. Another reason for such demands is that the resources available to support science and technology are limited, and thus choices must be made about priorities. Policy-makers thus expect that, to some degree, such choices should be made based on information about the relative benefits of different areas of science.

Scientists too justify their demands for public support by basing them on promises of benefits to society. For instance, in 1998 the US National Science Foundation adopted a second review criterion focused on societal impact in addition to its traditional criterion focused on scientific excellence. We see convergence between the conduct of scientific research and expectations for it to be useful or relevant. Some scientists have answered the call to be more useful or relevant to society by adopting a much more aggressive stance in political advocacy. Scientists are of course citizens as well as scholars, and are as free as anyone to express their political preferences. However, for the individual scientist, issue advocacy in the political process is not the only means of connecting science with society. Such advocacy has become so pronounced that some see the scientific community as a *cause* of political conflict. Paul Starobin (2006) wrote in the *National Journal*:

> the modern professional research scientist is not, by any stretch, a blameless figure – in this tale, that scientist emerges as an increasingly partisan and self-interested figure . . . the science community, even if at times a reluctant warrior, is itself contributing to the polarization that afflicts America's political culture. Viewed by the Founders as part of the glue that binds American democracy, the scientist is in danger of becoming a force for its increasing fragmentation.

But scientists need not always choose to engage the broader society as political advocates. As Chapter 1 asserts, scientists have a range of choices for how they act in the context of decision-making. To understand the different roles that scientists might play in decision-making it is thus important to distinguish policy and politics.

Even if all policy-making necessarily involves politics, sometimes politics and policy come into conflict. That is, the process of bargaining, negotiation, and compromise can get in the way of making commitments to particular courses of action. This matters when decisions are needed to increase the certainty of valued outcomes. To make the distinction between policy and politics more concrete, consider a September 2002 op-ed in *The New York Times* by US Representative Dick Gephardt (D-MO) on the debate over the possibility of United States intervention in Iraq. Representative Gephardt wrote that the decision whether or not to go to war in Iraq "is a case that deserves to be made on the basis of policy, not politics" (Gephardt 2002).

What did he mean by distinguishing policy and politics? In his op–ed Representative Gephardt expressed concern that President George W. Bush and members of his administration were using the decision on the war in Iraq as a means of consolidating the Republican Party's hold on government. He provided several examples to justify his concern, including, "In a recent speech in Kansas, Vice President Dick Cheney also entered the act, saying that our nation's security efforts would be stronger if a Republican candidate for Congress were elected" (2002: A31). Representative Gephardt concludes:

> Military action, if required, may meet with quick success in Iraq, but a peaceful, democratic Iraq won't evolve overnight. It will take the active support of both parties in Congress over the long term if we are going to win the peace. That's only going to happen if we act, not as Democrats or as Republicans, but as Americans. (2002)

In other words, it is in the national interests to reconcile the competing perspectives of Republicans and Democrats through practical actions, and not simply via the consolidation of power by one group or the other.

Whether or not the Bush administration was in fact seeking political advantage through the debate over Iraq, it is clear that Representative Gephardt was concerned about the consequences associated with a debate that focused on the relative power positions of competing political parties but excluded consideration of alternative courses of action in Iraq. Political power is of little policy utility if there are no good options available for decision-making.

The reality is of course that the politicization of policy is unavoidable and in fact desirable. We want conflicts to be resolved through the political process, which is much better than any of the alternatives. But politicization, when taken to such an extreme that it overshadows considerations of policy, can also threaten effective decision-making when those engaged in conflict over alternative courses of action evaluate those alternatives solely according to the gains or losses they provide to a group's ability to bargain, negotiate, or compromise relative to its opponents. Thus, the actual merits of alternative courses of action are at risk of being lost in a debate that becomes politicized to the extent of overshadowing policy. Ultimately, decisions matter because decisions shape real-world outcomes. Under some circumstances, politicization places at risk the connection between the policy and the outcomes that are supposedly being pursued through adoption of the policy.

Politics without policy threatens the democratic process for two reasons. First, it may lead to a limited participation in processes of decision-making, as some groups might be excluded. Second, political power can do little to serve common interests if there are no good alternatives for action available for decision-makers.

If politicization refers to situations where politics overshadows policy, then what about situations in which considerations of policy overshadow politics? Politicization has a counterpart which results when those engaged in conflict act as if all political debate can be resolved through evaluation of policy alternatives by some objective, scientific criteria. Such a perspective is consistent with the notion of the Science Arbiter introduced in Chapter 1 and reinforced by situations such as that faced by the Russian pilot in which information did in fact compel a particular course of action. Attempts to turn all policy-making into technical exercises that obviate the need for political debate have been called *technocracy* or *scientization* (see, e.g., Jasanoff 1990; Weingart 1999). Examples abound of contemporary political debates which invoke a technocratic vision of policy-making when the onus of decision-making is placed upon the shoulders of experts under an expectation that reliance on these experts will eliminate the need for politics. An example can be found in debates in the United States in 2005 and 2006 over the provision of emergency contraception in drug stores. Those wanting to see the drug made available cited a Food and Drug Administration's expert panel recommendation on the drug's safety as necessarily compelling that the drug be made available. At the same time, opponents of making the drug available sought experts who would impeach the safety of the drug. Of course the reality is that the debate reflected the values that are at stake in abortion politics. In the end the US government decided to make the drug available to women over the age of eighteen, reflecting a political compromise similar to establishing legal drinking ages. Given the challenges of politics in a charged issue such as abortion, it is no surprise that the technocratic vision is most appealing in highly contested political issues that involve considerations of science.

In such cases we often expect *science* – the systematic pursuit of knowledge – to provide insight into the nature of problems, decision alternatives, and their consequences with respect to desired outcomes. With respect to decisions, the technocratic impulse suggests that the reduction of scientific uncertainty necessarily leads to a reduction of political uncertainty. In other words, technocrats believe that by seeking a clearer conception of the relationship of alternative courses of action and their outcomes, there will necessarily be greater consensus on what action is preferable. We see such calls in most every area where science is contested, with notable recent examples including global climate change, genetically modified organisms, and nuclear waste disposal. For instance, in the case of emergency contraception, in 2005 the *New York Times* expressed a technocratic impulse when it wrote that the US government's decision at that time to keep the drug off the market meant that "politics or ideology was allowed to trump science" (*New York Times* 2005). In situations of political conflict about the means or ends that a policy is to achieve, politics will always and necessarily "trump" science simply because science does not compel action.

The politicization of science and the scientization of politics are mutually reinforcing. When politicians look to scientists to provide information that will help them to overcome or avoid politics, the result is inevitably more funding for research and more science conducted. More science results in more papers and more reports that invariably provide more material for those who seek to use science as a resource for negotiating for desired outcomes. As is typical of complex issues, science is frequently uncertain and diverse enough to provide ample material to sustain the arguments of competing political perspectives (Sarewitz 2000). Peter Weingart has written that "the competition for the latest, and therefore supposedly most compelling, scientific knowledge drives the recruitment of expertise far beyond the realm of consensual knowledge right up to the research frontier where knowledge claims are uncertain, contested, and open to challenge" (Weingart 1999: 158). And the circle is completed when contested knowledge claims result in demands for more science to "reduce uncertainty."

Chapter recap

This chapter has sought to address two questions:

- *Can science compel action?*

Yes, but only in particular circumstances characterized by shared values and low uncertainties about the relationship of alternative courses of action and those valued outcomes. By contrast, many issues in which scientists are asked to play a role in facilitating decision-making are complex, even more complex than the decision contexts faced by the Russian pilot or women resolving whether or not to get a mammogram. They share the following characteristics:

- The scope of choice is ambiguous and continuous, and competing interests work to limit the scope of choice.
- Considerable conflict exists about the desirability of different outcomes, because there are many outcomes and many interests.

- Considerable ambiguity exists not only about the relationship between alternative actions and desired outcomes, but about the conditions that motivate the need for decision-making in the first place.
- And more information promises little insight into the course(s) of action likely to lead to a desired outcome; in some circumstances more information may increase the ambiguity about the relationship between alternative actions and desired outcomes.

In these cases not only is there *uncertainty* about the nature of problems and the effects of actions in the face of problems, but uncertainty is also a resource for various interests in the process of bargaining, negotiation, and compromise in pursuit of desired ends. Of course, in some cases uncertainly may also facilitate democratic decision-making by allowing for ambiguity that enables competing interests to reach agreement on action. For instance, the effects of future climate change are not known with precision, so there is some risk that any particular decision-maker might suffer future harm. If the winners and losers associated with future climate change were to be known precisely, there might be less incentive for future winners to participate in a collective response. Consequently, there may be greater room for political compromise when winners and losers are unknown or at risk, that is, when uncertainty is present.

- *What are "policy," "politics," and "science"?*

Simply put, a "policy" is a decision; "politics" is bargaining, negotiation, and compromise in pursuit of desired ends; and "science" is the systematic pursuit of knowledge.

Decisions that we make about science, i.e., *science policies*, matter a great deal. Such decisions include what we decide to research, how many resources to devote to that research, who conducts it, how it is governed, how we structure its institutions, the expectations that we have for its connections with the needs of decision-makers, criteria for its success, and so on. Such decisions also will shape how science connects to policy-makers, and the degree to which scientific results have the potential to play a constructive role in policy-making.

Why should scientists seek to make better sense of science in policy and politics? Because, more than ever, science and scientists are being asked by society to play an important role in decision-making. Science matters for how we make decisions. And decisions matter for real-world outcomes – who benefits at whose expense, who (or what) lives or dies, how they live and how they die. Decisions cannot be avoided. And because outcomes – things we care about – are necessarily affected by decisions, it is only logical to explore the degree to which good decisions can be made more reliably more often and bad decisions avoided. Science, well used, holds great potential to improve life on earth. Science, poorly used, can lead to political gridlock, bad decisions, and threaten the sustainability of the scientific enterprise. The difference depends upon how we decide to use science in policy and politics. And that decision depends on being able to distinguish the different roles that scientists and other experts can play in policy and politics.

FOUR

Values

This chapter builds on the discussion in Chapter 3 of science in policy and politics by asking one question:

- What are the implications of different degrees of values consensus in decision contexts for the role of science in policy and politics?

The chapter answers this question through an extended "thought experiment" – an exercise in the imagination – that describes decision contexts that share some surface similarities, but suggest vastly different roles for science and expertise in the actual process of decision-making. Thought experiments allow the thinker to create carefully constructed, hypothetical scenarios in order to highlight aspects of the real world that are typically difficult to see or somehow obscured. Politics and policy are concepts that are often conflated and difficult to distinguish, making it difficult to understand the role of science in decision-making.[1] The thought experiment introduced below uses two scenarios to highlight the importance of the context of decision-making as a critical factor that shapes the interconnections of science, politics, and policy. This chapter builds upon the more general discussion of science and decision-making in Chapter 3 to explore in some detail the importance of political context for how we think about the role of science in decision-making.

Abortion Politics and Tornado Politics

The significance of information in decision-making, and the types of information that are significant for decisions, are a function of political context – specifically, science plays a different role in situations of values consensus and low uncertainty than in the opposite circumstances.[2] Consequently, for scientists to contribute to effective decision-making requires understanding the political context of a particular decision situation.

Imagine that you are in an auditorium with about fifty other people. Perhaps you have gone to hear a lecture or you are at a neighborhood meeting. As you entered the auditorium you noticed a thunderstorm approaching, but you paid it little attention. All of a sudden someone bursts into the room and exclaims that a tornado is fast approaching and that we must quickly proceed to the basement. Whatever formal event was going on is quickly transformed into several dozen hurried conversations, some expressing doubt, and the excited packing of purses and briefcases. As the milling about continues, someone shouts loudly to all in the room, "We must decide what to do!"

How might such a decision be made? For the purposes of this thought experiment, it is not unreasonable to assume that the people threatened by the tornado have a shared common interest in preserving their own lives.[3] Thus, to reach a consensus to commit to a course of action – say, stay in the auditorium and continue the meeting or go down to the basement – they would need to know if the tornado is indeed quickly coming this way. To collect this knowledge they might log on to the internet to find a real-time radar image, or just look out the window. If the tornado is indeed approaching the building then it is easy to imagine that the group would quickly decide to move to the basement. The essential point of this example is that for the group in the auditorium, under these idealized circumstances, a commitment to a specific course of action can be resolved primarily through the systematic pursuit of knowledge, i.e., science.

Let's call the process of bargaining, negotiation, and compromise in such situations *Tornado Politics*. Information plays such a critical role in Tornado Politics because participants in the decision-making process share a common objective – in this case the goal of preserving one's life – and the scope of choice is highly restricted – stay or go. We will return to Tornado Politics shortly, but first consider a very different sort of politics.

Imagine that you are in the same auditorium with the same group of fifty people, but, in this case, instead of deciding whether or not to evacuate, the group is discussing whether or not to allow abortion to be practiced in the community. For simplicity sake, let's just consider abortion generally, yes or no, and not in cases of medical necessity, etc.[4] One person stands up and exclaims, "The practice of abortion violates my religious beliefs and therefore must be banned in our community!" The next speaker states with equal passion, "The community has no right to dictate what can or cannot occur inside a woman's body. The practice of abortion must remain legal!" As the murmur of dozens of conversations grows louder, someone shouts loudly to all in the room, "We must decide what to do!"

How might such a decision be made? For the group in the auditorium to commit to a course of action – to ban or to allow abortion in the community – they might follow some sort of established procedure, such as a vote. They might form two groups (e.g., pro-life and pro-choice) and assign representatives to negotiate an outcome. Or if negotiations go badly they might even take up arms against one another to settle the matter by force. They may even cease attempting to live together as one community. There are clearly many ways in which such a decision might be made.

One strategy that is extremely unlikely to lead to a resolution on this issue is to systematically pursue knowledge about abortion in the same manner that was proposed in the case of the approaching tornado. Why? On this issue among the group there is not a shared commitment to a specific goal; to the contrary, there are conflicting commitments based on differing values. And while information matters in this situation, arguably no amount or type of *scientific* information about abortion can reconcile the different values. Even so, perhaps the community's overarching commitment to live under shared governance might lead to a desire to work together to achieve a legitimate outcome where all agree to live under the decision, once made. In such situations, let's call the process of bargaining, negotiation, and compromise *Abortion Politics*.

The idealized examples of Tornado Politics or Abortion Politics help create a language that will allow us to investigate the complexities and the challenges of making decisions with and about science.

Table 4.1 contrasts the different roles and characteristics of information in decision-making in Tornado and Abortion Politics. On the one hand, in Tornado Politics scientific information is critical for decision-makers to evaluate and compare decision alternatives. The information that is needed to make an effective decision lies outside of the room, hence the methods and perspectives of science are strengths in obtaining useful knowledge. This is very much the logic that underlies calls for scientific assessments designed to provide information to policy-makers. A fundamental assumption in such cases is that once everyone obtains a shared level of understanding a preferred course of action will become obvious and non-controversial. In the case of a rapidly approaching tornado, this is undoubtedly true. The decision faced by the Russian airline pilot is an instance of Tornado Politics.

On the other hand, in Abortion Politics, information certainly is important, but the relevant information is not scientific information about abortion. Information that might be shared in this case might

TABLE 4.1: *Roles and characteristics of information in decision-making*

Tornado Politics	Abortion Politics
Evaluation	Rationalization
Used to help assess decision alternatives	Used to help justify decision commitments
Comprehensive	Selective
Rational	Emotional
Logical	Narrative
Enlightenment	Power
Technocracy	Pluralism

be experiential in the form of narratives or anecdotes, or even information about how others view the issue. Information matters in this scenario, but it plays a very different role in decision-making than in the case of Tornado Politics. A decision in this case will result from the exercise of power in a decision-making system, and information will be used in an attempt to convince those sharing in the exercise of power to align with particular perspectives.

But within the context of Abortion Politics there is a strong desire to frame political conflict in terms of the dynamic of Tornado Politics. So, for example, those who have attempted, thus far unsuccessfully, to establish a scientific linkage between abortion and breast cancer help to make the general point that Abortion Politics is not about scientific information. Such efforts reflect a desire to turn Abortion Politics into Tornado Politics, to position the debate in the context of values that are widely shared (health) rather than in the context of those values which are not widely shared (pro-life *vs.* pro-choice).

In Table 4.1, the roles and characteristics listed under Tornado Politics are similar to how we might describe scientific information, whereas those listed under Abortion Politics are quite contrary to conventional descriptions of scientific information. Because our society values scientific information so highly, its characteristics are often portrayed in a positive light and are presented as being authoritative, and information with non-scientific characteristics is portrayed in a correspondingly negative light. For example, no scientist wants to see his/her work described as "emotional" or "selective." But, "comprehensive," "logical," and "rational" are positive attributes, whether the information being described is scientific or not. This is one reason why advocates of different political views agree on the need for policy to be based on "sound science" or "scientific integrity."

But a fundamental lesson of the thought experiments is that neither Tornado Politics nor Abortion Politics presents a "better" means of decision-making, but that the different types of politics arise from the context of decision-making. Similarly, the role of information in one scenario versus another cannot be judged to be a "better" strategy, as each is appropriate for the context. This perspective is well understood by many advocates whose job it is to promote particular political positions.[5]

For example, in March 2003, *The New York Times* reported on a memo prepared by a Republican Party strategist discussing the party's approach to the environment (Lee 2003). The memo offered the following advice, as presented in the article:

- The term "climate change" should be used instead of "global warming" because "while global warming has catastrophic connotations attached to it, climate change suggests a more controllable and less emotional challenge."
- "Conservationist" conveys a "moderate, reasoned, common sense position" while "environmentalist" has the "connotation of extremism."
- "Be even more active in recruiting experts who are sympathetic to your view and much more active in making them part of your message" because "people are more willing to trust scientists than politicians."

Kim Haddow of the Sierra Club, a group with positions usually at odds with the Republican Party, said that the memo's "advice is right.

It's very smart – confounding, troubling, but smart." It is "smart" because the guidance in the memo for the presentation of environmental information is appropriate for the context of political debate – in this case, Abortion Politics.

A real-world example of a situation that evolved from Tornado Politics to Abortion Politics is the contested 2000 presidential election (Sarewitz 2001; see also 2004). The selection of the US president on Election Day is typically a very straightforward process that exemplifies the dynamics of Tornado Politics.

Vote.

Count the votes.

The candidate with the most electoral votes wins the election. This is clearly a case of Tornado Politics, where the relevant information is the number of votes cast for each candidate, collected comprehensively and rationally, under a widely shared agreement that selecting a legitimate winner is a valued outcome of the election. But, in 2000, with the electoral votes just about equal in forty-nine states, the election in Florida was so close that it was unclear who had received more votes. Whoever won Florida would win the presidency. The candidates quickly proposed alternative means for resolving the uncertainty:

Count only these votes.

No, count these.

Finish by Friday.

Take as long as is needed.

Count the hanging chads.

What is a hanging chad?

Revote here.

Revote there.

Take it to court.

The systematic pursuit of information mattered less and less, and supporters of both George W. Bush and Al Gore sought to manipulate the process in such a way that would result in their candidate being elected. The situation evolved from one in which everyone had a shared interest in a legitimate outcome under the rules, to one in which the rules themselves were being debated based on the political advantage they would give to either candidate. Ultimately, as we all know, the election was decided by the Supreme Court.

Daniel Sarewitz (2000) asks if the election could have been resolved through science, "Suppose we had asked a team of scientists – rather than the US Supreme Court – to determine the winner of the Florida presidential election . . . Could such an approach have worked?" His answer is no,

> because uncertainty does not cause conflicting values. As a political matter, the direction of causation is quite the opposite: uncertainties emerge because the value conflict – an election, an environmental controversy – remains politically unresolved. Conversely, once a value conflict is settled through political means, the underlying uncertainties effectively disappear. The Supreme Court is a legitimate means for achieving this end; a team of scientists is not. (2000)

In the case of the 2000 election, thank goodness that the US Constitution has mechanisms for resolving disputes played out as Abortion Politics, not because of the outcome of the election, but because there was a legitimate outcome at all. An approach based on Tornado Politics (i.e., trying to precisely count the votes) may have led to greater uncertainties in who received more votes (e.g., what counts as a vote anyway?), proving that in some cases information is simply incapable (just as in the case of Abortion Politics) in resolving a dispute over values. Often, wars and conflict result where the mechanisms of Abortion Politics are not considered as legitimate as are decisions rendered by the US Supreme Court.

Now let's take the thought experiment a step further. Imagine if in the tornado example the group in the auditorium decided to adopt the mechanisms of Abortion Politics as the means for making a decision. That is, instead of seeking to assess the location and path of the tornado, they decided instead not to gather information and they held a vote. This is almost so absurd as to be nonsensical. To disconnect the decision from the circumstances of the tornado is to invite a tragic outcome – such as was the fate of the Russian pilot or at best a good outcome determined only by chance.

Conversely, imagine if in the abortion example the group were to adopt Tornado Politics as the means for making a decision. Here as well, one's thought experiment capabilities are pushed to the limit in trying to imagine what scientific study could conceivably be undertaken that would lend any useful information to this decision process.[6] But this dissonance illustrates a central point of the thought experiment: In the idealized tornado case, scientific information matters. In fact, in the very simple example presented here the information determines the decision. In the abortion case, scientific information matters not at all, and its pursuit would represent a distraction from the task of reconciling different value commitments through bargaining, negotiation, and compromise. As Daniel Sarewitz writes, "not only is there nothing wrong with the consequent messiness [of democratic politics], but all historical indications suggest that there is no viable alternative in a society that values freedom and justice and seeks to balance individual rights with the collective good" (2000).

Conflation, often willful, of Abortion and Tornado Politics encourages the mapping of established interests from across the political spectrum onto science and then uses science as a proxy for political battle over these interests. As Herrick and Jamieson observe, "the imprimatur of science is being smuggled into deliberations that actually deal with values and politics" (Herrick and Jamieson 2000: 15). An example of this dynamic has occurred in the United States in the debate over embryonic stem-cell research.

The issue of stem cells is controversial because – just as their name implies – embryonic stem cells come from human embryos, which may have been cloned for research purposes. Predictably, the use of embryos that are destroyed in the process of embryonic stem-cell research has caught the attention of anti-abortion/abortion rights advocates, who count among their ranks President George W. Bush. In October 2001, President Bush announced a policy that would prohibit the destruction of any embryo for use in federally funded stem-cell research, and limited scientists to research on existing lines (White House 2001a).

President Bush admitted that there may be potential benefits from embryonic stem-cell research, but he refused to compromise his principles to realize those benefits, no matter how large those benefits may be. For President Bush stem cells are an issue to be dealt with through the mechanism of Abortion Politics, and there is apparently no scientific information on the potential benefits of stem-cell research to alter his views.

By contrast, during the 2004 presidential campaign, Senator John Kerry characterized the stem-cell issue in a way that among those who share his perspective on the morality of stem-cell research was much more consistent with the notion of Tornado Politics. For example, in a speech Senator Kerry argued, "By supporting stem-cell therapy, we have the possibility to control the future. Not only can we reduce the economic cost of health care, we can reduce the emotional and social cost to families" (US Newswire 2004a). Kerry evidently believed that the potential benefits of embryonic stem-cell research justified going forward with research, under the assumption that many people share his belief that stem-cell research ought to be evaluated in terms of costs and benefits. Among those who have decided that stem-cell policy should be guided by a calculation of the costs and benefits of health care and are unmoved by arguments to restrict stem-cell research, scientific information is critically important because it provides a basis for evaluating the trade-offs between the costs and benefits associated with different courses of action.

Confusion about the role of science in the stem-cell debate arises when those sharing President Bush's perspective and those sharing Senator Kerry's perspective fail to understand not just each other's perspective, but the fact that they are engaged in fundamentally different types of politics. For example, the forty-eight Nobel laureates who endorsed John Kerry did so in part because they believe that the Bush Administration has placed "unwarranted restrictions on stem-cell research" that are impeding medical advances (Scientists and Engineers for Change 2004). The laureates seem to have assumed that the issue is in fact about medical advances. But for many people who share the views of President Bush, this argument would appear to miss the point. Senator Kerry made a similar case for stem-cell research in a June 2004 radio address: "Believe it or not, there was a time when some questioned the morality of heart transplants" (US Newswire 2004b). In other words, Kerry seemed to believe that it would only be a matter of time before everyone recognized that the benefits of stem-cell research outweigh any costs. That is, the issue will eventually become a matter of Tornado Politics where values are widely shared. If so, once everyone sees the tornado coming, the correct course of action will be obvious and generally accepted.

In his August 2001 address to the nation on stem-cell research, the president justified his decision to limit research to then-available stem-cell lines as follows:

> My position on these issues is shaped by deeply held beliefs. I'm a strong supporter of science and technology, and believe they have the potential for incredible good – to improve lives, to save life, to conquer disease. Research offers hope that millions of our loved ones may be cured of a disease and rid of their suffering. I have friends whose children suffer from juvenile diabetes. Nancy Reagan has written me about President Reagan's struggle with Alzheimer's. My own family has confronted the tragedy of childhood leukemia. And, like all Americans, I have great hope for cures. I also believe human life is a sacred gift from our Creator.[7] (White House 2001a)

For President Bush the issue was not a scientific issue at all, because no matter what scientists or those who rely on scientific information say about potential benefits, this information is highly unlikely to change his position. Five years after announcing his initial policy, President Bush vetoed legislation that would have allowed federal funding of embryonic stem-cell research.

Some scientists who support federal funding for stem-cell research have sought to use science to develop "ethically acceptable" approaches to stem-cell research, e.g., research that does not require the destruction of embryos. They are seeking to move the debate from Abortion Politics to Tornado Politics by removing the basis for the values disputes over stem-cell research. So far, such an approach has instead backfired from the standpoint of the political interests of these scientists because it begins by granting that the issue is indeed a matter of Abortion Politics – in other words, it begins by accepting that research that destroys embryos is unethical. In at least one prominent case an effort to develop such "ethically acceptable" stem-cell research was accompanied by an embarrassing overstatement and misrepresentation of what science has achieved, leading Senator Arlen Spector (D-PA), a strong supporter of stem-cell research, to comment, "It's a big black eye if scientists are making false and inaccurate representations" (Weiss 2006). The *American Journal of Bioethics* asked, "Can't we just be honest and say that we favor embryonic stem cell research, at least for now . . . even though the research destroys embryos?" (Weiss 2006).

The stem-cell issue cannot be resolved through appeals to science, but instead through the process of politics. Efforts to turn the stem-cell debate into a matter of Tornado Politics have arguably done more than just failed to secure federal research funding, they have given a black eye to the broader scientific enterprise. So long as there is dispute over values in a particular context, appeals to science can offer little to resolve those values differences, and may instead transform scientific debate into political debate.

Chapter recap

This chapter has addressed one question:

- *What are the implications of different degrees of values consensus in decision contexts for the role of science in policy and politics?*

Figure 4.1 shows how the highly idealized notions of Tornado and Abortion Politics map onto the framework of the roles of science in policy and politics presented in Chapter 2. In a situation characterized by a broad consensus on values, admittedly an imprecise characterization, science and scientists have great potential to play a positive role in providing scientific information without necessarily engaging such information with action alternatives, that is, as Science Arbiters or Pure Scientists. By contrast, in a situation characterized by values conflict, policy advocates typically seek to use scientific information as a means of arguing for one course of action over another. Hence, the relationship of science to alternative courses of action is more

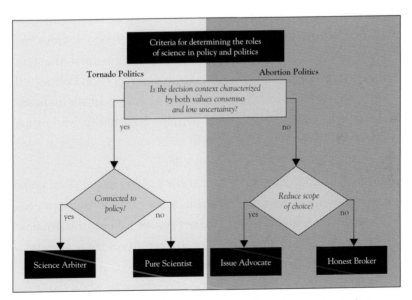

Figure 4.1 The idealized realms of Tornado and Abortion Politics

effectively clarified when science is explicitly associated with choice, either through issue advocacy or honest brokering of policy alternatives.

In reality, unlike carefully constructed thought experiments, decisions, particularly those involving contested environmental issues, take on characteristics of Tornado and Abortion Politics simultaneously. In such situations the following circumstances often apply. Alternative courses of action materially affect outcomes. To some degree, scientific information matters for understanding both the motivation for the decision and the consequences of alternative courses of action. At the same time, different perspectives and values shape commitments to alternative courses of action. There may be fundamental, irreducible uncertainty about the problem and policy options. Knowledge itself may be contested. And there may be a lack of shared values on both ends and means. In such contexts it is important to accurately assess what science can and cannot do as a contribution to the democratic process.

In the language of this chapter, the effectiveness of science in decision-making will vary considerably, to the extent that a particular decision context exhibits characteristics of Tornado Politics and Abortion Politics. In many situations, just as what seems in the stem-cell debate, elements of Tornado Politics and Abortion Politics will occur simultaneously as those seeking to scientize debate frame the issue in terms of information and perhaps uncertainty, while those seeking to politicize the debate will emphasize the values disputes and perhaps the consensus on knowledge.

It is important to recognize that those seeking to politicize policy debates that involve science hold the trump card. So long as there is a dispute over values, the issue will necessarily take on the dynamics of Abortion Politics, irrespective of the actions of those seeking to scientize the debate.

The strategies of Tornado Politics are effective when there is a broad consensus over values. In other words, scientists and scientific institutions are likely to be effective as Pure Scientists or Science Arbiters only in those cases where there is a broad agreement on values. Where no such agreement exists, science offers much less prospect of contributing to effective decision-making. Even worse, in cases where significant values conflicts exist, efforts to serve as Pure Scientists or Science Arbiters are likely to foster the politicization of science. If values conflicts cannot be avoided, then one might still hold out hope that uncertainty somehow can be reduced or eliminated, in order to clarify the role of science in decision-making, and if nothing else to delineate available options and their consequences. In later chapters we shall see such strategies at work in the cases of environmental politics and debate over the decision to go to war in Iraq. Often, the effect of efforts to characterize situations of Abortion Politics as Tornado Politics is to bring issue advocacy into the realm of Science Arbiters and Pure Scientists. If this were not complicated enough, in addition to disputes over values, another characteristic of decision processes that it is important to clarify in order to improve understandings of science in policy and politics is uncertainty, which is the focus of Chapter 5.

FIVE

Uncertainty

This chapter seeks to answer four questions:

- What is "uncertainty"?
- Why is it that some equate the reduction of scientific uncertainty with an increased likelihood of reaching a political consensus?
- Why is scientific uncertainty fundamentally irreducible in some contexts?
- Why does uncertainty matter in how we think about science in policy and politics?

There are several answers to the first question to be found in the scientific literature, and they share a common characteristic. The answer to the second question lies in a conflation of different types of uncertainty. The answer to the third question lies in an appreciation of the nature of science in the context of a complex world. Efforts to reduce uncertainty through scientific research often have the exact opposite effect of increasing uncertainty. The answer to the fourth question builds on the arguments developed in the previous chapters that information by itself does not compel a particular decision. The reduction of scientific uncertainty does not necessarily compel a political consensus.

What is "uncertainty"?

Uncertainty means that in a particular situation more than one outcome is consistent with our expectations. An "outcome" simply refers to an actual situation (i.e., some realized or true condition) in the past, present, or future, such as the number of whales in the ocean, the current temperature you feel on your skin as you read this sentence, or the roll of a dice. This definition of uncertainty encompasses each of the conventional understandings of uncertainty used by academics in terms of ignorance, risk, and measurement and estimation. We make decisions in an effort to manage uncertainty, yet the presence of uncertainty both complicates and facilitates achieving a political consensus. Consequently, how we view uncertainty and its relationship to decision-making shapes our approach to science in policy and politics.

Uncertainty, in the view of economist John Maynard Keynes, is a fundamental condition of all human life (Skidelsky 2000).[1] For Keynes uncertainty represented a state of mind:

> By "uncertain" knowledge . . . I do not mean merely to distinguish what is known for certain from what is only probable. The game of roulette is not subject, in this sense, to uncertainty . . . The sense in which I am using the term is that in which the prospect of a European war is uncertain, or the price of copper and the rate of interest twenty years hence, or the obsolescence of a new invention . . . about these matters, there is no scientific basis on which to form any calculable probability whatever. We simply do not know! (Keynes 1937: 213–14)

Some scholars who study decision-making further distinguish situations of "ignorance" as described by Keynes ("we simply do not know") from situations of "risk" in which we know the probability distribution of possible outcomes, such as with the roll of a die. Ignorance can only be reduced with the passage of time and through the actual unfolding of events. By contrast, we can often improve our qualitative or quantitative understandings of risk through the systematic pursuit of knowledge.

Many scientists and engineers define uncertainty somewhat differently than Keynes. They define uncertainty as a distribution of values around a measurement or estimate. For example, the US government's National Institute of Standards and Technology defines uncertainty as a "parameter, associated with the result of a measurement, that characterizes the dispersion of the values that could reasonably be attributed to the measurand" (NIST Physics Laboratory 2006).[2] Such "measurements" can take the form of direct observations or indirect estimates of physical quantities, such as the height of Mt. Everest, the number of whales in the ocean, or the concentration of carbon dioxide in the atmosphere. And measurements and estimates can also take the form of virtually constructed quantities such as the output of computer models. Such quantities could refer to conditions (or outcomes) in the past (e.g., the temperature of the earth 10,000 years ago as estimated from tree rings), present (e.g., the temperature of your oven as you prepare to cook dinner), or the future (e.g., the prediction of tomorrow's temperature). For scientists and engineers, uncertainty is to be quantified and, if possible, reduced through new knowledge. From this perspective the goal of science "to advance knowledge" is synonymous with the notion of "reducing uncertainty."

Scholars who study uncertainty often find themselves grappling with deep issues of epistemology and ontology (Gillies 2000). Does uncertainty exist outside our perceptions? Is the world deterministic or contingent? Thankfully, for present purposes resolution of these deeper philosophical questions is unnecessary. Irrespective of the fundamental nature of the universe, in concrete situations where time and other resources are finite, decisions necessarily must be made under conditions of uncertainty (Hammond 1996).[3] That is, irrespective of whether or not uncertainty is a human construct or an intrinsic feature of nature, people inevitably must make decisions when more than one outcome is consistent with their expectations.

Of course, people's expectations often turn out to be poorly correlated with actual outcomes. Along these lines, Kenneth Hammond describes a useful distinction between subjective and objective uncertainty:

> A person betting on a horse race may be highly (subjectively) uncertain about whether the horse on whom the bet is riding will win, but in fact the race may be fixed – determined in advance – so that a certain horse *will* win; thus subjective uncertainty may be high although objective uncertainty is almost zero. The opposite conditions may also occur; the bettor may be highly confident about which horse will win (low subjective uncertainty) even under conditions of high objective uncertainty (all horses of equal handicap, running an honest race). (Hammond 1996: 14)

Objective uncertainty thus refers to a complete and accurate characterization of the entire set of outcomes associated with a particular set of expectations. Subjective uncertainty, by contrast, refers to our judgments about how to characterize the entire set of outcomes associated with a particular set of expectations.

There are situations where we have very limited means to assess objective uncertainty. In other situations we have no means to evaluate objective uncertainty. For example, Keynes argues that we have no basis for knowing the price of copper twenty years hence. Based on everything that we know (and Keynes would argue, everything that we can now know), in twenty years the price of copper – an outcome – could be greater, less, or the same as today. Because uncertainty is a human quality I might be completely certain that the price of copper twenty years from now will be between $2 and $3 per kilogram while you may be equally certain that the price will be between $1 and $5 per kilogram, with each value in this interval having an equal probability. In terms of the number of possible outcomes, you are more uncertain than I because you see 401 possible outcomes (i.e., $1.00, 1.01, 1.02 . . . $5.00) whereas I expect only 101 (i.e., $2.00, $2.01 . . . $3.00), but because the future will unfold in only one way, there is no objective way to reconcile these differing expectations.

In some situations uncertainty can be objectively measured. Such systems are usually closed systems, such as are found in a laboratory experiment, or can be treated as if they are closed. Consider the roll of two fair dice. In this instance we have complete certainty about the distribution of outcomes; that is, we know that the sum of numbers on the two dice will lie between two and twelve. And based on our understandings of probability we can know with complete certainty the frequency of number combinations that we should expect. But even with this objective understanding we cannot know in advance the specific outcome for a single roll, even though we know that some outcomes are more likely than others. We are uncertain because more than one outcome is consistent with our understanding, but we can implement decision strategies (e.g., a wager) in a manner which maximizes the correspondence of our understandings of subjective uncertainties with our understandings of objective uncertainties. But despite our best efforts, uncertainty in most decision situations is not like the roll of a die, and consequently our understandings of uncertainty are often themselves uncertain.

Now consider scientific measurement and estimation. Here as well, uncertainty can be fruitfully defined as more than one outcome being consistent with understandings. For every quantitative measurement or estimate some error is associated with that quantity. More generally, measurement errors may result in the process of measurement from mistakes made by humans (e.g., a transcription mistake) or by computers (such as a false identification of a whale by a computer algorithm based on sonar patterns). Errors may also result from the consequences of statistical sampling, the limitations of our ability to measure quantities precisely, or a lack of accuracy in variables used as inputs to the calculation of a particular measurement. Because all measurements have errors, error analysis is an important aspect of research.

For example, in the nineteenth century the height of Mt. Everest was estimated to be 29,002 feet above sea level (Wright 2000). At the turn of the century another survey resulted in an estimate of 29,141 feet. In the 1950s a subsequent series of measurements were averaged to arrive at 29,028 feet, a number that found its way into geology textbooks for decades. In 1999, scientists using Global Positioning Satellite technology estimated the height to be 29,035 feet plus or minus 7 feet. The remaining uncertainty results from limits in the precision of the technology, uncertainties in precisely knowing sea level at Everest's location, the seasonal snowpack, and the fact that Everest is growing at a few millimeters per year due to tectonic forces. Scientists have bounded their uncertainty, but more than one outcome remains possible for the height of Mt. Everest. Uncertainty means that more than one outcome is consistent with our understandings.

Why do some equate the reduction of scientific uncertainty with an increased likelihood of reaching a political consensus?

In the context of decision-making, scientific research is frequently justified in terms of providing a perspective on the objective uncertainty present in particular decision situations. While science can provide accurate characterizations of objective uncertainties in a range of situations, for almost every issue of significant political debate, from climate change to the presence of weapons of mass destruction in Iraq, science is limited to providing a rigorous, formalized expression of subjective uncertainties. In other words, most descriptions of objective uncertainties are highly subjective. Stated more strongly, there are no such things as objective uncertainties except in fully characterized, closed systems, such as are found in games of chance such as poker and dice, or controlled laboratory experiments.

The confusion of objective and subjective uncertainties was behind the famous failure of Long Term Capital Management (LTCM), a hedge fund whose 1998 collapse threatened the entire global financial system. The source of the failure was the assumption by LTCM's managers that they had objectively characterized uncertainty associated with international finance. They believed that their understanding of the behavior of financial markets encompassed all possible outcomes. Events proved that their characterization of uncertainty did not encompass the events that actually transpired. "Long-Term was so self-certain as to believe that the markets would *never* – not even for a wild swing some August and September – stray so far from its predictions . . . Dice are predictable down to the decimal point; Russia is not; how traders respond to Russia is less predictable still" (Lowenstein 2000: 234–235).[4]

The concepts of subjective and objective uncertainty are critical for understanding scientific and political debates involving all areas of science. For example, in 2003 several scientists published a paper that estimated that in historical times the North Atlantic was home to 865,000 Minke, Fin, and Humpback whales (Roman and Palumbi 2003). They reported a 95 percent confidence interval of between 581,000 and 1,297,000 whales. What does this mean? This means that more than one outcome is consistent with the paper's methods – their estimate is uncertain. Based on their assumptions, data, and methods, the paper estimates between 581,000 and 1,297,000 whales in the ocean before whaling began. If one accepts as true (or certain) the assumptions, data, and methodology employed by these researchers then within this context their results provide a description of objective uncertainty. But of course the study's assumptions, data, and methods reflect subjective choices, each clouded by uncertainties. Thus, to the degree that one has questions about the certainty of the paper's underlying assumptions, data, and methodology, instead of providing a definitive statement of the objective uncertainty associated with the number of whales in the ocean, the results are a highly formalized expression of subjective uncertainty.

Consequently, it should come as no surprise that the 2003 study of historical whale populations was contested by other scientists, who favor different methods and assumptions. The journal *Nature* reported the views of several experts with different perspectives on historical whale populations (Clarke 2003). One expert said that the study's findings were "completely out of the realm of reality," and another explained, "Estimates of genetic diversity are complicated and error-prone" (Clarke 2003). Absent a time machine and technology to perform a complete oceanic census of whale populations, we must rely on the methods and perspectives of science to clarify our subjective uncertainties. Put another way, there can be no objective certainty on the question of how many whales inhabited the ocean in historical times. So long as there exist (or, more generally, the possibility exists for) different, valid scientific perspectives, some degree of uncertainty will always exist (Sarewitz 2000).

Debates among scientists about the uncertainty associated with various processes or variables take on added significance when, as is often the case, decisions are linked to the scientific debate. For example, a news story described the implications thus, "If stocks were really much larger in the past, new hunts could be delayed by the International Whaling Commission until the whale population builds closer to original levels. The commission says hunting should not be allowed until the population reaches at least fifty-four percent of the ocean's carrying capacity for the mammals" (Schmid 2003). Not surprisingly, an interest group that promotes the sustainable harvesting of whales and other natural resources judged the scientists' work to be problematic and then engaged in an ad hominem attack on one of its authors (IWMC 2003). An environmental interest group viewed the study quite differently, receiving the study as "music to whale-conservationists' ears, as it emphasized that the toll of whaling was far worse than anyone had suspected" (Cetacean Society International 2003). Uncertainty thus becomes an issue of importance for policy and politics. In pursuit of desired outcomes through policies, different people and different groups seek to shape perceptions of uncertainty in ways that lend advantage to their perspectives. Struggles over scientific uncertainty can easily become very political. Value disputes that are best handled by the mechanisms of Abortion Politics often become scientized by one side or another in order to suggest that the values disputes can be resolved through a reduction of scientific uncertainties utilizing the mechanisms of Tornado Politics.

Daniel Sarewitz (2000) argues that expectations for science to resolve political conflict almost always fall short because science provides an "excess of objectivity" useful in supporting a broad range of conflicting subjective positions.

> Rather than resolving political debate, science often becomes ammunition in partisan squabbling, mobilized selectively by contending sides to bolster their positions. Because science is highly valued as a source of reliable information, disputants look to science to help legitimate their interests. In such cases, the scientific experts on each side of the controversy effectively cancel each other out, and the more powerful political or economic interests prevail, just as they would have without the science. This scenario has played out in almost every environmental controversy of the past 25 years.

Given the diversity of views on the implications for action of most scientific topics, even those where some form of scientific consensus may exist, entrenched interests need not produce "junk science" when they have a wide selection of credentialed scientists to choose from in support of their positions. In spite of vigorous differences of political opinion among combatants in each of these issues, without exception they share the belief that science is the appropriate battleground, under the assumption that if a perception can be created that science is on your side, you win.

As a result, science is often used as a strategic and tactical resource in ideological debate. That advocates of particular positions "spin," cherrypick, or even misuse information to present their preferred action in the best light is a staple of political debate and, as such, is not particularly problematic for either science or politics. Such politicized science always has been and always will be an inherent component of the political process. One stretches scientific claims at the risk that it will harm their own credibility and cause.

For some observers, a greater danger for both science and politics occurs when members of the scientific community itself participate in the politicization of science, particularly through the media. The consequences are described by Arthur Kantorwitz: "In the resulting media contest between competing authorities, it is not possible to tell whether science or politics is speaking. We then lose both the power of science and the credibility of democratic process" (Kantrowitz 1994: 101). Loss of the power of science matters only if science, or more accurately the information provided through science, has in some cases a unique role to play in the policy process. For if information does not matter, then distinguishing science and politics would be of little concern; we could all then simply invent "facts" as convenient.

Uncertainty can be used to describe not only information, but processes of decision-making as well. Barry Burden, a Harvard political scientist, observes, "humans worry about their decisions for one reason: they are uncertain" (Burden 2003: 6). Of course, this perspective is also what underlies the old adage that "ignorance is bliss." Why? Because ignorance is accompanied by a lack of uncertainty, it is also accompanied by a corresponding lack of worry. Thomas Gray explained this in 1747 in the last verse of his poem, "Ode on a Distant Prospect of Eton College," that gave us the phrase "ignorance is bliss":

> To each his suff'rings: all are men,
>   Condemn'd alike to groan,
> The tender for another's pain;
>   Th' unfeeling for his own.
> Yet ah! why should they know their fate?
>   Since sorrow never comes too late,
> And happiness too swiftly flies.
>   Thought would destroy their paradise.
> No more; where ignorance is bliss,
>   'Tis folly to be wise. (Gray 1747)

Ignorance's bliss usually doesn't last for very long. Because we constantly find ourselves in John Dewey's "forked-road situations" we face a multitude of choices about how to act, about which fork in the road to take. Not choosing, or choosing poorly, can lead to undesirable outcomes. Consequently, we strive to lift the veil of ignorance that obscures complete understanding of the consequences of our alternatives courses of action. In other words, we try to ensure that our subjective estimates of uncertainty correspond with an objective ideal.

As discussed in Chapter 3, we seek to reduce uncertainty about the future in preferred directions when we make decisions as individuals and in groups. When groups make decisions, the choice is typically reflective of a political process requiring some sort of compromise. Making a decision also means *not committing* to all available alternatives to that particular course of action. For instance, when the Russian pilot discussed in Chapter 3 decided to send his plane into a dive, he was eliminating the possibility of a rapid ascent or of doing nothing. His hope was that by reducing his available choices to a single option he and his passengers would survive. In the process of decision-making we seek to make some desired outcomes more certain, and other, less desirable outcomes, less certain. Decision-making generally, and policy-making specifically, is the process of managing uncertainty. Good decisions reduce uncertainty about desired outcomes in preferred directions.

The management of uncertainty is possible because we have some ability to understand the consequences of selecting one fork in the road over another. As Harold Lasswell and Abraham Kaplan wrote in 1950, "Decision-making is forward looking, formulating alternative courses of action extending into the future, and selecting among alternatives by expectations of how things will turn out" (1950: xv–xvi). If we had absolutely no ability to associate alternative courses of action with their consequences, then the process of decision-making would not matter, as we would have no basis for selecting one fork in the road over another.

As happened in the case of Long-Term Capital Management, bad decisions can result when scientists or decision-makers misunderstand the uncertainty that they face and underestimate the range of possible outcomes associated with their understandings. Of course, the opposite situation can also be the case, such as when scientists or policy-makers misunderstand uncertainty in the form of overestimating the range of outcomes associated with their understandings. A good example of this can be seen in estimates of the National Aeronautics and Space Administration (NASA) of the likelihood of the catastrophic loss of the space shuttle before the Challenger and Columbia disasters. In both cases hindsight shows that NASA dramatically overestimated the odds of a successful launch.

Even as we make decisions to manage uncertainty, decision-making is made more complicated because outcomes associated with particular decisions are themselves uncertain in a number of respects. A decision may not have the intended effects. A decision may have unexpected consequences, including the opposite of those desired in making the decision in the first place. Consider the efforts in the early 1990s by policy-makers in Mexico City to improve air quality by imposing a regulation that limited travel on some days to cars with license plates that end in even numbers and on other days to odd numbers.[5] Both policy-makers and policy analysts expected to reduce the number of cars on the road and consequently to improve air quality. The policy was adopted and air quality got worse. Why? Many people simply bought another vehicle so that they would have two cars, one with a license plate ending in an odd number and another with an even number. Typically the second car was a junker, with dirty emissions. The analysts' understanding of uncertainty (i.e., the range of possible outcomes associated with the policy), with hindsight, was seriously in error.

A central theme that emerges from experience is that important decisions are often clouded by inherent uncertainty and, in many instances, efforts to reduce uncertainty paradoxically have the opposite effect.[6] Frequently, research results in the discovery that the vast complexities associated with phenomena that evolve slowly over long periods – such as those associated with the integrated earth system – were in fact previously underestimated, thereby having the effect of expanding uncertainties (Sarewitz et al. 2000). F. David Peat argues that the great scientific and technological advances of the twentieth century resulted not in increasing certainty, but the opposite. "The ways we represent the world, in everything from language to art and science, deeply influence the ways we structure our world and understand ourselves. During the twentieth century many of these means of representation underwent change from certainty to uncertainty, and today our world is more tentative and open to doubt and uncertainty" (2002: 97–98). In a decision setting, this can have the perverse effect of increasing political controversy rather than reducing it, a situation which ironically can lead to calls for even more research to reduce uncertainties, while the original problem motivating the research in the first place goes unaddressed.

Efforts to manage uncertainty become even more complicated in the context of groups with diverse interests. Policy-making invariably involves groups with different perspectives on desired outcomes, on the connection of various policy alternatives, and their expectations for the consequences of those alternatives. So even as different groups are each trying to reduce uncertainties through decision-making, they are typically trying to reduce them in different directions, i.e., in ways that more closely approximate their desired outcomes. Thus, an inescapable aspect of decision-making as the management of uncertainty is the struggle over "who gets what, when, and how." Policy-making is inherently a political process, and both politics and policy are focused on dealing with the fundamental uncertainties of human life.

Why is scientific uncertainty fundamentally irreducible in some contexts?

Why is there uncertainty at all? Why can't we know precisely how many whales inhabited the ocean in historical times? Why can't we eliminate ambiguity between decision alternatives and their consequences? Uncertainty results from three characteristics of life: chance, myopia, and intentionality.

Chance

Consider the poker game known as five card draw.[7] In a standard fifty-two-card deck there are a total of 2,598,960 possible five card poker hands. Let us assume that in your hand you hold a pair. What are the odds that by exchanging the other three cards you will draw a third card to match the pair? In this instance you can know with great precision that over the long run in 71.428 % of such situations you will fail to improve your hand. Thus, when you exchange three cards you are "uncertain" about the outcome that will result, but you can quantify that uncertainty with great certainty.

This sort of uncertainty is that associated with random processes, that is, one in which each element of a set (in this case a deck of cards) has an equal chance of occurring. Because we know the composition of the deck and the set of possible events (i.e., the relative value of dealt hands), it is possible to calculate precisely the uncertainty associated with future events. Scientists call this *aleatory* uncertainty and it is studied using mathematical statistics (Hoffman and Hammonds 1994). Such uncertainty, by definition, cannot be reduced. One can never divine what the next card will be, although one can precisely calculate what one's chances are of receiving a particular card. Similarly, in predictions associated with the sciences there is also irreducible uncertainty associated with the nature of random processes, such as we find in the familiar case of forecasts of the weather a few days into the future.[8]

Myopia

But let us take the poker example a step further. Assume that you find yourself playing cards with a less-than-honest dealer. This dealer is adding and removing cards from the deck so that the deck no longer has the standard fifty-two cards. The process is no longer *stationary* – it is changing over time. If you were to know the cards added and removed, i.e., to have the ability to quantify the changing composition of the deck, to quantify uncertainty, you would simply need to recalculate the probabilities based on the new deck of cards. But if you were unaware that the deck was changing in its composition, then you could easily miscalculate the uncertainty associated with your options. Similarly, if you were aware that the deck was changing, but were not privy to the exact changes, you would be unable to calculate precisely the uncertainty (but would know that the assumption of a standard fifty-two card deck could be wrong). This sort of uncertainty is called *epistemic* uncertainty and is associated with incomplete knowledge of a phenomenon – and incomplete knowledge of the limits of one's knowledge (Hoffman and Hammonds 1994).

Unlike aleatory uncertainty, epistemic uncertainty can in some cases be reduced through obtaining improved knowledge. In the case of the changing deck of cards uncertainty could be reduced using several methods. For instance, one could carefully observe the outcome of a large number of hands and record the actual frequencies with which particular hands occur. For instance, if four aces were added to the deck, one would expect to be able to observe the results in the form of more hands with ace combinations. Of course, the more subtle the change, the more difficult it is to detect.[9] An alternative approach to understanding uncertainty would be to build a model of the card substitution process. This would require some sort of knowledge of the underlying dynamics of the card substitution process. Such knowledge might include the use of a known scientific "law" or observed relationship. For instance, research might reveal that the number of cards added to the deck is proportional to the number of players at the table. With such knowledge, a quantitative model of the poker game can be created and the model can be used to generate understandings of the uncertainty associated with various outcomes. The more one understands about the card replacement process, the better understanding one can have about the associated uncertainties. But if the process of changing cards were continuous (i.e., highly non-stationary or variable), then based on the observations of hands dealt one might develop numerous equally plausible theories about the changing nature of the probabilities. Unless one could discover the pattern underlying the change process (in effect "close" the system[10]) then such theories would be subject to continuous revision as experience unfolds.

But even though epistemic uncertainty can in principle be reduced, if one is dealing with open systems (as is almost always the case when one deals with human or natural systems) the level of uncertainty itself can never be known with absolute certainty. Seismologists assigned a probability of 90 percent to their 1988 prediction of the Parkfield earthquake for the period 1988–93, but the expected earthquake did not occur until 2005 (see Nigg 2000; Savage 1991; Sieh et al. 1989). Were the scientists simply confounded by the unlikely but statistically explicable one-out-of-ten chance of no earthquake? Or was their probability calculation simply wrong, i.e., because more outcomes were possible than the scientists expected?

Our myopia can sometimes be corrected, but sometimes it cannot and in some cases we cannot even know if after applying a correction our view is any clearer at all.

Intentionality

Purposive decision-making also introduces an element of uncertainty. Humans have the ability to change outcomes. When the US Supreme Court ruled in favor of George W. Bush in the disputed 2000 election, that decision led to one man being elected instead of another, with many consequences ever since. Had the Supreme Court ruled in Al Gore's favor the consequences would have been equally large, and very different. Because outcomes are contingent on our decisions, we are able to act with intention. One of the consequences of the ability to make decisions is uncertainty. Peter Bernstein writes that "uncertainty makes us free . . . Our decisions matter. We can change the world. Whether that change turns out to be for better or worse is up to us" (1996: 229–230).

Climate change: a case study in the conflation of political and scientific uncertainties

The case of climate change offers a wonderful example of the dynamics described in this chapter. On the one hand, there are those who argue that a scientific consensus (i.e., low uncertainty) on the causes and consequences of human emissions of greenhouse gases should compel a particular course of action on climate change, typically regulation of greenhouse gas emissions. On the other hand, there are those who argue that scientific uncertainties are so large that we should not regulate greenhouse gases. In both cases, competing Issue Advocates with different vested interests have decided that their desire to limit the scope of choice will best be served by waging a political battle through science. Of course, the basis for opposition for most of these folks has nothing to do with scientific uncertainty and everything to do with their valuation of the costs and benefits of taking action.

For example, George W. Bush stated his opposition to action on climate change in 2001, "For America, complying with those [Kyoto] mandates would have a negative economic impact, with layoffs of workers and price increases for consumers" (White House 2001b). Even though the basis for President Bush's opposition is grounded in how he values expected outcomes, he nonetheless raised scientific uncertainty about climate itself as a basis for his decision:

> we do not know how much effect natural fluctuations in climate may have had on warming. We do not know how much our climate could, or will change in the future. We do not know how fast change will occur, or even how some of our actions could impact it. For example, our useful efforts to reduce sulfur emissions may have actually increased warming, because sulfate particles reflect sunlight, bouncing it back into space. And, finally, no one can say with any certainty what constitutes a dangerous level of warming, and therefore what level must be avoided. (White House 2001b)

But his invocation of such uncertainties is just a distraction. Consider that during the 2004 presidential election Senator John Kerry, who also opposed the Kyoto Protocol, never invoked scientific uncertainty as the basis for his opposition (he claimed the fact that developing countries did not participate in the treaty as the basis for his opposition). Because Bush and Kerry shared opposition to Kyoto but had different views on the science of climate change, it suggests that one's views on climate science are not deterministic of one's political perspectives.

Yet, while there is ample evidence that scientific uncertainty is not the main reason behind opposition to action on climate change, advocates of Kyoto and emissions reduction policies more generally have seized upon claims of near-absolute scientific certainty as the linchpin of their advocacy efforts. In this way, the political debate over climate change takes place in the language of science, with some invoking "scientific uncertainty" as the basis for their preexisting ideological and political views, and others invoking "scientific certainty" (often in response to those invoking "scientific uncertainty"). In the climate debate, claims of uncertainty map onto one political agenda and claims of certainty onto another political agenda. In climate politics there is no such thing as objective or unbiased science, it is all viewed through the lens of the political conflict. The great irony here is that the debate of certainty and uncertainty is largely disconnected from the real reasons for political debate over climate change, which is based on a conflict over values. The climate issue is an example of Abortion Politics cloaked in the guise of Tornado Politics.

If this assertion is close to being right, it means that opponents of action on climate change already will have taken a big step toward winning the political debate when advocates of action invoke certainty as the basis for action. When opponents of action raise scientific uncertainty as a reason for delay or inaction, advocates of action spend considerable time and effort trying to disprove allegations of uncertainty as the centerpiece of their efforts, but no matter how well they make their case for certainty, it can do little to change the underlying political outcome, as the opponents can just switch their justification to something else while maintaining their political commitment to opposition. Further, in making claims to certainty in science it is easy for Issue Advocates to overstretch in their claims, such is often done in the frequent linkage of the latest weather disaster to greenhouse gas emissions, which occurred following Hurricane Katrina and during the heat waves of the summer of 2006.

What is typically overlooked in situations of political conflict being waged through science is that options are neither fixed nor given. Action on climate change is typically cast as a yes or no decision on a single option, such as the Kyoto Protocol. But science also has an important role in contributing to the invention of new and innovative policy options, i.e., to create more forks in the road. New options can change political calculations and motivate new coalitions and thus opportunities for political compromise and policy action. Paradoxically, efforts to expand choice can sometimes lead to more effective decision-making by creating opportunities for competing factions to find agreement instead of gridlock or conflict.

As an example of policy options on climate change that might allow for consensus, consider so-called "no-regrets" policies. Much has been made about the actions taken by localities in the United States and international corporations to reduce greenhouse gas emissions. But such actions are not simply the result of sacrifices made today for benefits decades hence. Instead, as political scientist Michele Betsill at Colorado State University has found,

> motivating local action to mitigate global climate change calls for an indirect strategy, focused on the ways in which emissions-producing activities are embedded in broader community concerns since the emphasis is on how reducing greenhouse gas emissions can help the city address other (more pressing) problems [such as air pollution or high energy costs], questions of the scientific basis for climate change rarely come up. When and if they do, city officials can easily reply that these are actions they should take anyway. (2001: 404)

And consider how Jeffrey Immelt, CEO of GE characterized his company's actions: "We are investing in environmentally cleaner technology because we believe it will increase our revenue, our value and our profits . . . Not because it is trendy or moral, but because it will accelerate our growth and make us more competitive" (2005: 5).

Pragmatic "no-regrets" interventions tied to clear short-term benefits such as reducing dependence on Middle Eastern oil, advancing economic competitiveness, and reducing particulate air pollution may offer a more effective path to reducing greenhouse gas emissions. Because the benefits of such policies will be felt in the near term, they build a strong basis for continued efforts in the future, and are thus robust to considerations of certainty or uncertainty. And, of course, a similar argument can be made about responding to the impacts of climate change, where efforts to reduce vulnerability to disasters will have a clear pay-off in the short term. In this manner, scientific uncertainty need not stand in the way of political action. Progress can be made toward achieving widely shared outcomes – energy efficiency, national security, and resiliency to risks – with little need to resolve competing views of the science of climate change or its implications for the future.

Chapter recap

This chapter has sought to answer three questions:

- *What is "uncertainty"?*

Uncertainty means that in a particular situation more than one outcome is consistent with our expectations.

- *Why is it that some equate the reduction of scientific uncertainty with an increased likelihood of reaching a political consensus?*

Science is about advancing knowledge, which is often interpreted as being synonymous with the notion of reducing uncertainty. Decision-making is about reducing another kind of uncertainty – that associated with the outcomes associated with choice. It is therefore very easy for some to come to the conclusion that reducing uncertainty about the world – through science – will clarify what actions to take in a particular situation. In some cases, such as the situation experienced by the Russian airline pilot described in Chapter 3, information does compel a particular action. But as Chapter 4 described, where there is fundamental conflict over the values at stake, scientific information offers little prospect of resolving a political dispute. Nonetheless, there exist strong incentives for all parties to act as if reducing scientific uncertainty compels a particular political outcome, to characterize a situation of Abortion Politics as Tornado Politics. At once such a strategy assumes a values consensus and invokes the authority and legitimacy of science as a tool for resolving disputes. Chapter 6 explores in more depth why some view science as compelling certain decisions.

- *Why is scientific uncertainty fundamentally irreducible in some contexts?*

And even if a reduction of scientific uncertainty compelled a particular political outcome, in some cases its reduction is simply impossible. This chapter discussed three reasons why this is so. First, there is considerable randomness or chance in the world that leads to perhaps quantifiable but irreducible uncertainty. Second, we have limited knowledge and perspective. Our view of the world, especially on timescales of decision-making, is myopic. Third, we have choices and choices can shape outcomes. We can take one fork in the road or another, and each will lead to different destinations. Because we have discretion, this introduces another element of uncertainty into the world.

Scientific uncertainty complicates the role of the scientist in decision-making. In cases where values are shared and uncertainty is either reducible or at least able to be characterized, then the scientist can play an effective role as a Pure Scientist or Science Arbiter. But in cases where values may be widely shared but uncertainty is large or growing through additional research, then a focus only on scientific uncertainty offers less to the decision-making process, as factors well beyond science will most likely be the most important factors in decision-making. In such situations the scientist may be more effective as an Issue Advocate or an Honest Broker.

SIX

How science policy shapes science in policy and politics

This chapter seeks to address one question:

- How do policies for science shape the role of science in policy?

One answer to this question is that the "linear model" of science creates incentives for scientists to present themselves as Pure Scientists or Science Arbiters when in fact they are acting as Stealth Issue Advocates, as will be described in detail in the case of *The Skeptical Environmentalist* discussed in Chapter 7. This chapter describes the origins of the linear model and how it creates incentives for stealth issue advocacy among scientists.

Chapters 4 and 5 argued that science is most likely to play an effective role in decision-making in situations characterized as having a consensus of values *and* low (or reducible) uncertainty, even as various interests turn to science as a strategy for advancing their political interests. If this conclusion is applicable more generally, then it suggests that of the four different, idealized ways that scientists could interact with decision-makers introduced in Chapter 1 – Pure Scientist, Science Arbiter, Issue Advocate, and Honest Broker – the first two are effective strategies for connecting science

TABLE 6.1 *Efforts to connect science to policy and politics under the linear model resulting in issue advocacy*

		View of science	
		Linear model	Stakeholder model
View of democracy	Madison	Pure Scientist	Issue Advocate
	Schattschneider	Science Arbiter	Honest Broker of Policy Options

and decision-making only under certain, fairly unique or prescribed circumstances. A more general conclusion then follows – the so-called "linear model" of the relation of science and society where consensus on science is a necessary and sufficient precursor to achieving a political consensus is not always (and less generously, perhaps rarely) an effective guide for scientists seeking to play a positive role in the policy-making process. Yet, the linear model exerts a strong hold on many scientists and policy-makers as a model for thought and action.

This chapter argues that contemporary *science policies* create strong incentives for scientists to wage political battles through science by emphasizing the roles of Pure Scientist and Science Arbiter in all cases, when in fact an advocacy position is actually being expressed. At the core of the argument presented here is a critique of the long-standing expectation that science can and should be separated from considerations of the applications of science. This expectation is reflected in the very language of science policy when we use concepts such as "basic research" and "applied research" to describe the work of scientists. It is difficult even to have a discussion of science in society without falling back on the terms "basic" and "applied." The linear model is not simply a rationale for explaining the influence of science in politics, but is in fact a strongly held worldview on how science ought to connect to its broader societal context (Bocking 2004; Sarewitz 1996; Stokes 1997). This chapter critiques this linear model and suggests an alternative perspective.

Ironically enough, much of the scholarship on the linear model has itself fallen victim to the pathologies of the linear model. Many scholars in the field of science and technology studies are well aware of its shortfall as a guide to action and have thus moved on to other, more contemporary subjects. Meantime, the vast majority of practicing scientists remain completely unaware of these critiques sitting in science studies journals. One reviewer of an early draft of this manuscript said that this chapter was unnecessary because "the STS audience knows all this stuff already." But as the case study on *The Skeptical Environmentalist* (Chapter 7) suggests, such knowledge, even if well appreciated by some, has yet to be fully appreciated among practicing scientists who continue to wage political battles under the logic of the linear model.

The linear model is a product of the underlying philosophy of science policy since World War II. But since the early 1990s science studies scholars have increasingly challenged this dominant paradigm.[1] In the early years of the twenty-first century it is unclear if or how a complete transition from one view of science policy to another might play out. But several trends already seem well established. First, the science policies that have shaped thinking and action over the past fifty years are unlikely to continue for the next fifty years. Second, decision-makers and society more generally have elevated expectations about the role that science ought to play in contributing to the challenges facing the world. Third, the scientific community nevertheless struggles to manage and meet these expectations. Together these trends suggest that more than ever there is a need for systematic thinking about science policy – that is, a science of science policy. Such research is central to developing new ways of thinking about, and ultimately utilizing, science in policy and politics.

What is "science policy"?

If "science" refers to the systematic pursuit of knowledge, and "policy" refers to a particular type of "decision-making," then the phrase "science policy" involves all decision-making related to the systematic pursuit of knowledge. Harvey Brooks (1964) characterized this relation as twofold. *Science for policy* refers to the use of knowledge to facilitate or improve decision-making. *Policy for science* refers to decision-making about how to fund or structure the systematic pursuit of knowledge.

Brooks' characterization of science policy has shaped thinking about science policy ever since, reinforcing a perception that science and policy are separate activities which are subject to multiple interrelations, rather than activities that are instead inextricably interconnected. But while Brooks' distinction has proved useful, reality is more complex, since the way we view science policy itself shapes the sorts of questions that arise in science policy debates. Science for policy and policy for science shape each other. Academics like to say that they are "co-produced."

Policy for science refers to decisions about the structure, functions, and priorities of science and how such decisions influence the kind of knowledge that will be available for decision-makers. Policy for science and science for policy are subsets of what might be more accurately described as a "policy for science for policy" (Pielke and Betsill 1997). To the extent that our thinking about science policy separates decisions about knowledge from decisions with knowledge in decision-making, it reinforces a practical separation of science from policy, and implies that we can make these two types of decisions independently of one another (Guston 2000).

The linear/reservoir model

Vannevar Bush's (1945) seminal report *Science – The Endless Frontier*, implied that in return for the privilege of receiving public support, the researcher was obligated to "produce and share knowledge freely to benefit – in mostly unspecified and long-term ways – the public good" (Office of Technology Assessment 1991: 4). One of the fundamental assumptions of post-war science policy is that science provides a reservoir or fund of knowledge that can be tapped and applied to national needs. According to Bush,

> The centers of basic research . . . are the wellsprings of knowledge and understanding. As long as they are vigorous and healthy and their scientists are free to pursue the truth wherever it may lead, there will be a flow of new scientific knowledge to those who can apply it to practical problems in Government, in industry, or elsewhere. (1945: 12)

Implicit in Bush's fluvial metaphor is the linear model of the relationship between science and the rest of society: basic → applied → development → application → societal benefit. This model posits that societal benefits are to be found "downstream" from the reservoir of knowledge. Others have described variations of the liner model as a "ladder," an "assembly line," and a "linked-chain" (Gomory 1990; Kline 1985; Wise 1985).

The linear/reservoir model is a metaphor explaining the relationship of science and technology to societal needs. It is used *descriptively* to explain how the relationship actually works and *normatively* to argue how the relationship ought to work. The linear model appears in discussions of both science policy, where it is used to describe the relation of research and societal needs (Brown 1992), and technology policy, where it is used to describe the relation of research and innovation (e.g., Branscomb 1992).[2] The linear model was based on assumptions of efficacy, and not comparisons with possible alternatives. In 1974, US Congressman Emilio Daddario, a member of the House Science

Committee, observed that members of Congress defer to the assertions of scientists that basic research is fundamental to the benefits society receives from investments in science "and *for that reason, if for no other*, they have supported basic research in the past" (Daddario 1974, emphasis added). So long as policy-makers and scientists felt that science was meeting social needs, the linear model was unquestioned.

The linear model posits that basic research, conducted by scientists who are largely autonomous, is a resource for applied research. Applied research is the source of results useful for practical concerns, including policy development. The terms "basic" and "applied" have thus become fundamental to discussions of science and society. For example, the US National Science Foundation in its annual report on "Science and Engineering Indicators" has used precisely these terms to structure its description of the taxonomy of science.

The notion of "basic research" and the linear model of which it is a part has been tremendously successful from the standpoint of the values of the scientific community. Not only did it present a compelling, utilitarian case for government support of the pursuit of knowledge, it also explicitly justified why "pure" research "deserves and requires special protection and specially assured support" (Bush 1945: 83). The special protection included relative autonomy from political control and standards of accountability determined through the internal criteria of science. In a classic piece, Polanyi (1962) sketched in idealized fashion how a "republic of science" structured according to the values of pure science provides an "invisible hand" pushing scientific progress toward discovering knowledge that would have inevitable benefits for society.[3]

The linear model and axiology of science

A value structure is part of any culture, and the culture of science is no different. More than thirty years ago, Alvin Weinberg (1970) suggested four explicitly normative "axiological attitudes" – statements of value – which scientists hold about their profession. Whereas Weinberg's concern was the physical sciences, such perspectives are broadly applicable to all aspects of science:

- Pure is better than applied.
- General is better than particular.
- Search is better than codification.
- Paradigm breaking is better than spectroscopy.

For Weinberg, these attitudes are "so deeply a part of the scientist's prejudices as hardly to be recognized as implying" a theory of value (1970: 613). But these values are critical factors for understanding both thinking about and the practice of science policy. And understanding why science policy is currently undergoing dramatic change requires an understanding of how Weinberg's theory of value, if not breaking down, is currently being challenged by an alternative axiology of science.

Understanding the context of modern science requires a brief sojourn into the history of science policy. In the latter part of the 1800s, scientists began to resent "dependence on values extraneous to science," in what George H. Daniels calls "the rise of the pure science ideal" (1967: 1703). The 1870s saw such resentment come to a head.

> The decade, in a word, witnessed the development, as a generally shared ideology, of the notion of science for science's sake. Science was no longer to be pursued as a means of solving some material problem or illustrating some Biblical text; it was to be pursued simply because the truth – which was what science was thought to be uniquely about – was lovely in itself, and because it was praiseworthy to add what one could to the always developing cathedral of knowledge. (1967: 1699)

Like many other groups during this era, the scientific community began to organize in ways that would facilitate the making of demands on government for public resources. Scientists had become an interest group. In the United States, scientists who approached government for support for research activities clashed with policy-makers who expressed the need for any such investments to be associated with practical benefits to society.

Expressing a value structure that goes back at least to Aristotle, scientists of the late nineteenth century believed that the pursuit of knowledge associated with the pursuit of unfettered curiosity represented a higher calling than the development of tools and techniques associated with the use of knowledge. Hence, the phrase "pure research" came to refer to this higher calling with "purity" serving as a euphemism for the lack of attention to practical, real-world concerns (Daniels 1967). The first editorial published in *Science* in 1883 clearly expressed a value structure:

> Research is none the less genuine, investigation none the less worthy, because the truth it discovers is utilizable for the benefit of mankind. Granting, even, that the discovery of truth for its own sake is a nobler pursuit. It may readily be conceded that the man who discovers nothing himself, but only applies to useful purposes the principle which others have discovered, stands upon a lower plane than the investigator. (1883: 1)

Some scientists of the period, including Thomas Henry Huxley and Louis Pasteur, resisted what they saw as a false distinction between "pure" and "applied" science (Huxley 1882: 7–30; Stokes 1995). And few policy-makers of the period saw the need for such a distinction. For them, utility was the ultimate test of the value of science (Dupree 1957). The late 1800s saw different perspectives on the role of science and society coexist simultaneously. But Weinberg's axiology of science emerged from the period as the value structure that would shape the further development of science policies in the first half of the twentieth century.

From pure science to basic research

Weinberg's axiology of science stressed the importance of basic research. The term "basic research" was not in frequent use prior to the 1930s. But after World War II the concept became so fundamental to science policy that it is difficult to discuss the subject without invoking the corresponding axiology. The notion of basic research arose in parallel with both the growing significance of science in policy and the growing sophistication of scientists in politics. By the end of World War II and the detonation of the first nuclear bombs, the acceleration of the development of science-based technology was inescapable. Throughout society science was recognized as a source of change and progress whose benefits, even if not always equally shared, were hard to dismiss.

The new context of science in society provided both opportunity and challenge. Members of the scientific community, often valuing the pursuit of pure science for itself alone, found themselves in a bind. Historically in the United States, the government valued science almost exclusively for the practical benefits that were somehow connected to research and development. Policy-makers had little interest in funding science at a level desired by the scientific community simply for the sake of knowledge production.

Government reticence to invest in pure science frustrated those in the scientific community who believed that, historically, advances in knowledge had been important, if not determining, factors in many practical advances. Therefore, the scientific community began to develop a "two birds with one stone" argument to justify its desire to pursue truth, and the demands of politics for practical benefits. The argument held that pure research was the basis for many practical benefits, but that those benefits (expected or realized) ought not to be the standard for evaluating scientific work. If practical benefits were used as the standard of scientific accountability under the US system of government, then science could easily be steered away from its ideal – the pursuit of knowledge.

The scientific community took advantage of the window of opportunity presented by the demonstrable contributions of science to World War II and successfully argued that US science policy should focus on basic research. The effect of this successful argument was to replace the view held by most policy-makers that science for knowledges sake was of no use, with the idea that *all research* could potentially lead to practical benefits. In the words of Vannevar Bush, the leading formulator of this post-war science policy perspective: "Statistically it is certain that important and highly useful discoveries will result from some fraction of the work undertaken [by Pure Scientists]; but the results of any one particular investigation cannot be predicted with accuracy" (1945: 19).

Central to this change in perspective was acceptance of the phrase "basic research" and, at least in policy and political settings, the gradual obsolescence of the term "pure research." The term "basic" came without the pejorative notion associated with lack of purity imputed upon practically focused work, because the term "basic" means in a dictionary-definition sense "fundamental," "essential," or "a starting point." Research that was "basic" could easily be interpreted by a policy-maker as being fundamental to practical benefits. The terms "basic" and "fundamental" are used interchangeably to describe research and carry multiple meanings. For many scientists "basic research" means "pure" research disconnected from application and for many policy-makers the phrase means "essential to application." These completely conflicting interpretations reflect an ambiguity that has become increasingly problematic since the end of the Cold War (Stokes 1997).

Basic research would be connected to societal benefits through the linear model of science. The linear model holds that basic research leads to applied research, which in turn leads to development and application (Pielke and Byerly 1998). To increase the output (i.e., societal benefits) of the linear model, it is necessary to increase the input (i.e., support for science). And the linear model shapes thinking about the role of science in a broader society. It recommends a division of labor in which scientists "do science" and others worry about the applications of science. Such thinking is not only invoked as science policy, but, in the context of specific policy issues, used to argue that scientists should serve as Pure Scientists or Science Arbiters in particular policy contexts.

At the macro-level the linear model suggests a design for science policies. Government invests in basic research, scientists do the research and make it available for decision-makers in industry and elsewhere throughout society. Scientists need not worry about the application or use of science as that occurs downstream. But the linear model also suggests a role for scientists at the micro-level of particular policy contexts. It suggests that scientists simply need to get the science right in order to help improve decision-making in particular contexts. Hence, in a wide range of political issues involving science one frequently hears scientists formally eschewing any discussion of policy or political context, invoking the role of the Pure Scientist or the Science Arbiter.

A good example of the invocation of the Pure Scientist can be found in the development of the US Global Change Research Program, a scientific research program designed to provide decision-makers with usable information related to climate change. That program was originally set up in 1989 as a basic research program, focused only on science. One of its leaders argued that a scientific focus in the program would serve the needs of global change policy: "Broad trust in the objectivity of science is essential for the success of policymaking efforts, particularly in international negotiations with far-reaching economic implications. Independent and objective science, therefore, serves both science and policy needs" (HCSST 1989: 99). Some politicians agreed, and Al Gore stated of the program, "more research and better research and better targeted research is (sic) absolutely essential if we are going to eliminate the remaining areas of [global change] uncertainty and build the broader and stronger political consensus necessary for the unprecedented actions required to address this problem" (SCCST 1989).

As evident in the quote from Mr. Gore, there is a close association between the linear model and the perspective discussed in Chapter 5 which holds that reducing scientific uncertainty leads to a political consensus. In case after case, both scientists and politicians assert that getting the science right is a precursor to forging a political consensus (Sarewitz 1996; 2004; Sarewitz et al. 2000). Such claims are not just a political strategy, but reflect the underlying philosophy of science policy and axiology of science that characterize post-World War II science policy.

Seeds of conflict: freedom versus accountability

From the perspective of the scientific community, from the pre-war to post-war periods, the concepts of pure research and basic research remained one and the same: the unfettered pursuit of knowledge. For the community of policy-makers, however, there was an important distinction; "pure research" has little to do with practical benefits but "basic research" represents the "fund from which the practical applications of knowledge must be drawn" (Bush 1945: 19). From the perspective of policy-makers, there was little reason to be concerned about science for the sake of knowledge alone; they had faith that just about all science would prove useful.

The different interpretations by scientists and policy-makers of the meaning of the term "basic research" have always been somewhat troubling (Kidd 1959). A brief review of the use of the term "basic research" by the scientific community finds at least four interrelated definitions of the phrase, as summarized in Table 6.2.

From the standpoint of policy-makers, basic research is defined through what it enables, rather than by any particular characteristic of the researcher or research process. These conflicting interpretations of basic research by policy-makers and scientists have coexisted for much of the post-war era, even as for decades observers of science policy have documented the logical and practical inconsistencies. René Dubos (1961: 1209) identified a "schizophrenic attitude" among scientists, succinctly described by George H. Daniels: "while

TABLE 6.2: *Four definitions of "basic" research*

By product:	Basic research refers to those activities which *produce* new data and theories representing an increase in our understanding and knowledge of nature generally rather than particularly (Armstrong 1994; National Science Board 1996).
By motive:	Basic research is conducted by an investigator with a *desire* to know and understand nature generally, to explain a wide range of observations, with no thought of practical application (National Science Board 1996).
By goal:	Basic research *aims* at greater knowledge and mastery of nature (Bode 1964; White 1967).
By standard of accountability:	The basic researcher is free to follow his or her own intellectual interest, to gain a deeper understanding of nature; and is *accountable* to scientific peers (Bozeman 1977; Polanyi 1962).

scientists claim among themselves that their primary interest is in the conceptual aspects of their subject, they continue to publicly justify basic research by asserting that it always leads to 'useful' results" (1967: 1700). It is this attitude that has allowed post-war science policy to operate successfully under the paradigm of the linear model, apparently satisfying the ends of both scientists and politicians. "Basic research" was the term used to describe the work conducted in that overlap. The situation worked so long as both parties – society (patron) and scientists (recipient of funds) – were largely satisfied with the relationship.

We see this schizophrenic attitude in situations where science plays a role in political debates. Scientists often claim to be focused only on science, while also making the case that their science is central to resolving political conflicts in one specific direction or another, representing a difficult pair of claims to manage as they can easily become contradictory. If a debate is really about science, then surely it can take place on the pages of seldom-read peer-reviewed journals. But if the debate is about more than science, then it would likely spill over into the media, the internet, and legislative chambers.

As discussed in Chapter 4, expectations for science to resolve political conflict almost always fall short because science often provides an "excess of objectivity" useful in supporting a broad range of conflicting subjective positions (Sarewitz 2000). In other words, the linear model of science creates conditions that foster the pathological politicization of science in those cases where science is called upon to arbitrate contested political issues. The scientific enterprise is diverse enough to offer information that can be used to support a diversity of perspectives on just about any subject, and in cases where there is little disagreement on values, scientific uncertainty is unlikely to be involved in any case. Decisions are rarely like that faced by the Russian airline pilot described in Chapter 3. They are instead clouded by a diversity of vested interests, various perspectives on relevant science, and even different views on whether or not science is in fact relevant to decision-making.

Concerns about the increasing politicization of science reflect that times have changed. Increasingly, neither scientists nor politicians are satisfied with the science policy of the post-World War II era. For instance, in 1998 the Science Committee of the US House of Representatives undertook a major study of US science policy under the following charge:

> The United States has been operating under a model developed by Vannevar Bush in his 1945 report to the President entitled *Science: The Endless Frontier*. It continues to operate under that model with little change. This approach served us very well during the Cold War, because Bush's science policy was predicated upon serving the military needs of our nation, ensuring national pride in our scientific and technological accomplishments, and developing a strong scientific, technological, and manufacturing enterprise that would serve us well not only in peace but also would be essential for this country in both the Cold War and potential hot wars. With the collapse of the Soviet Union, and the de facto end of the Cold War, the Vannevar Bush

approach is no longer valid. (US House of Representatives Committee on Science 1998: 5)

While the Congressional report acknowledged the need for a new science policy, it did not sketch out what that new policy might entail. However, an understanding of the tensions leading to calls for change suggests how science policy is changing.[4]

These tensions have long been recognized. Daniels (1967: 1704) sketches the tensions underlying the changing nature of science policy:

> The pure science ideal demands that science be as thoroughly separated from the political as it is from the religious or utilitarian. Democratic politics demands that no expenditure of public funds be separated from political . . . accountability. With such diametrically opposed assumptions, a conflict is inevitable.

And these tensions were recognized even earlier, in 1960, by the Committee on Science in the Promotion of Human Welfare of the American Association for the Advancement of Science: "science is inseparably bound up with many troublesome questions of public policy. That science is more valued for these uses than for its fundamental purpose – the free inquiry into nature – leads to pressures which have begun to threaten the integrity of science itself." (AAAS 1960: 69)

For many years under growing budgets in the context of the Cold War, post-war science policy successfully and parsimoniously evaded this conflict. Given pressures for accountability and more return on public spending, conflict is unavoidable.

Why, more specifically, did the United States post-war science policy go largely unchallenged for half a century?[5] From the point of view of society, it solved problems. First, science and technology were key contributors to victory in World War II. Infectious diseases were "conquered." Nuclear technology ended World War II and promised power "too cheap to meter" (Strauss 1954). From the point of view of the scientific community, most good ideas received federal funding. The United States economy dominated the world. As a consequence of this changing context, there was less pressure from the public and their representatives on scientists for demonstrable results; there was less accountability. Scientists, policy-makers, and the broader public were largely satisfied with national science policies.

But at the beginning of the twenty-first century policy-makers face many new challenges. Some infectious diseases have rebounded through resistance to antibiotics, and new diseases, such as SARS and bird flu, threaten health. For many, the cost of healthcare makes world-leading medical technology unaffordable. The events of September 11, 2001 show the risks to modern society at the intersection of fanaticism and technology. The availability of weapons of mass destruction makes these risks even more significant. New technologies, in areas such as biotechnology and nanotechnology, create new opportunities but also threats to people and the environment. Many problems of the past have been solved, but new ones are with us, and science and technology are often part of both the problem and possible solutions. The question of how to govern science and technology to realize benefits to society is thus more important than ever.

At the same time, many scientists are unhappy as budgets are not keeping pace with research opportunities; as the scientific community has grown and knowledge has expanded, the number of proposed research ideas exceeds available funding to support them. In the United States, the National Institutes of Health underwent a five-year doubling of their budget in the early 2000s only to subsequently see many scientists and researchers voice vociferous complaints when funding increases inevitably slowed from this unsustainable rate of growth. Strong global competition and demands for political accountability create incentives for policy-makers to support research with measurable payoffs on relatively short time scales, while within the scientific community competition for tenure and other forms of professional recognition demand rigorous, long-term fundamental research. As the context of science changes, scientists share anxieties with others disrupted by global economic and social changes.

While scientists perceive their ability to conduct pure research constrained by increasing demands for practical benefits, policy-makers simultaneously worry that basic research may not address practical needs. Because consensus on post-war science policy has weakened, discussion of science policy has moved beyond the partial overlap of motives that helped sustain post-war science policy. Scientists now speak of their expectation of support for pure research and policy-makers increasingly ask for direct contributions to the solution of pressing social problems. Many scientists see this as an open invitation to engage in the political process using their expertise as a political resource. But this dynamic creates the very conditions, explored in the previous chapters, that lead to a conflation of Abortion and Tornado Politics, and ultimately the waging of political battle through science. It is important for scientists to recognize the influence of the linear model for how they choose to engage the broader society, and to recognize that they have chose beyond the Pure Scientist and Science Arbiter that follows so naturally from the logic of the linear model. The linear model is not the only way that science might relate to decision-makers.

How the linear model fosters stealth issue advocacy among scientists

Let us return to discussing more general implications of the linear model for shaping science in policy and politics, and possible alternatives. To introduce an alternative, consider a thought experiment. Imagine a world that formalizes the implications of the linear model, in which science is not formally connected to stakeholders but is provided to decision-makers only through established political institutions, such as political parties (Pielke 2002: 368). In the United States, scientists would be categorized by whether they belonged to the Democratic or Republican parties, in Great Britain by membership in Labour, Conservative, Liberal Democrat parties, etc. Scientific journals as well (peer reviewed no doubt) would be published through the party structures, e.g., *Labour's Nature* and *Republican Science*. Public funding for research would be provided to political party organizations, which would then disseminate resources as they saw fit, perhaps relying on traditional peer review, but with no expectation that the research would be anything other than the pure pursuit of curiosity.

Would there be any problem with such a structure? It would be difficult to find any practicing scientist who would advocate structuring the scientific enterprise in such a manner. Indeed the time-honored practices of peer review and other mechanisms of insulating science from politics seek to avoid the direct influence of politics on science. One reason for the high esteem in which science is held is its independence from overt political influence. But ironically, the linear model of science fosters circumstances much more like the imaginary world described above than many would like to admit. The linear model of science encourages the mapping of political interests onto science, and in the process encourages a morphing of political and scientific debate.

Chapters 4 and 5 provided criteria under which the linear model is most appropriate as a guide for thinking about the relationship of science and decision-making. These criteria are a high level of consensus over values to be achieved by decision-making and low uncertainty. Under such conditions the Pure Scientist or Science Arbiter is more likely to contribute effectively to decision-making. Of course a corollary to this guidance is that absent values consensus and low uncertainty the scientists seeking to act as a Pure

Scientist or Science Arbiter greatly enhances the opportunities for "stealth issue advocacy." Stealth issue advocacy refers to situations in which one claims to be serving as a Pure Scientist or Science Arbiter, but instead is focused on reducing the scope of choice available to decision-makers, which is the defining characteristic of an Issue Advocate. The typical strategy of the Stealth Issue Advocate is to seek to reframe as Tornado Politics an issue that is more accurately characterized as Abortion Politics. Because most scientists are trained in the axiology of the linear model, some approach the use of science in decision-making only as Pure Scientist or Science Arbiter.

Of course, recognizing the criteria under which the linear model makes the most sense as a guide to a more effective relationship between science and decision-making should not preclude particular scientists from stepping into the political arena as Issue Advocates in cases where they feel strongly enough. But they should do so in full recognition that there are choices to be made about what role they might play in policy and political processes. And they certainly should not hide their advocacy behind the façade of the linear model.

To the extent that the pervasive culture of the linear model in the scientific enterprise fosters stealth issue advocacy, it helps to explain why there is a paucity of guidance provided by scientists to policy-makers seeking to expand the range of available policy alternatives – serving as Honest Brokers of Policy Alternatives. Yet by contributing to the creation of new "forks in the road," science still holds untapped potential to defuse political debate (and gridlock) by contributing to identification of choices not seen and paths not taken, rather than just adding ammunition to opposing sides entrenched in political battle. When used as a general guide to science in decision-making the linear model can in fact diminish opportunities for science to contribute effectively to policy, and create conditions that serve to bring politics into science.

Science policy research can help to document and evaluate the use of science in policy in highly political contexts. Of particular use would be evaluations of a wide range of institutions around the world that work at the interface of science and policy in highly political contexts. Examples of institutions that have adopted variations of the Honest Broker of Policy Alternatives as their manner of relating scientific information to decision-makers include Enquete Commissions in Germany and several other European countries, the Office of Technology Assessment in the United States, and the Technology Foresight Knowledge Pool in the United Kingdom (Bimber 1996; Georghiou 1996; Krohn 2005). Their experiences, both successes and failures, are well worth evaluating.

The most frequent response from scientists to observations that science has become more political is a call for a retreat to the familiar confines of Pure Science. But if science is to contribute to decision-making, such retreat is simply not advisable, as other modes of interaction make better sense in contexts of values conflict and high uncertainty (that is to say, the characteristics of most public issues involving science). The scientific community should thus indeed maintain its involvement in contested political issues rather than withdraw, as was historically the case when scientists sought to be "value free" and removed from practical concerns. It makes no sense to try to return to a bygone – and largely mythical – era when science was thought to be separate from politics.

Stealth issue advocacy poses threats to the scientific enterprise. If the public or policy-makers begin to believe that scientific findings are simply an extension of a scientist's political beliefs, then scientific information will play an increasingly diminishing role in policy-making, and a correspondingly larger role in the marketing of particular political agendas. This will be tragic because not all politics are Abortion Politics – society has a wide range of issues on which there are widely shared values and an opportunity for science to contribute knowledge to helping to realize those values – scientific information often matters a great deal. The lure of the linear model is strong, as is the corresponding tendency to couch issue advocacy in the guise of Pure Science or Science Arbiter, as Chapters 7 and 8 will show.

SEVEN

Preemption and the decision to go to war in Iraq

Information is a resource in politics and policy. Information can indicate that a problem compels action. For example, while conducting research into the effects of supersonic airplanes on the atmosphere, scientists serving as Science Arbiters investigating the effects of the stratospheric exhausts of space vehicles and supersonic airplanes learned that a commonly used family of chemicals long thought to be benign – chlorofluorocarbons (CFCs) – had the potential to damage the ozone layer that helps to protect life on earth. These research results created political uncertainties where previously there was none – for decades CFCs were widely used because they appeared to be inert. The new results suggested that action might be needed to deal with an environmental threat. This information put CFCs on the agenda of government and industry decision-makers (see Andersen and Madhava Sarma 2002).

Information also can show that the policies advocated by one group are more apt to lead to desired outcomes than policies advocated by another group. For example, when industrial scientists conducted research to develop cost-effective substitutes for CFCs in the early 1980s, their research expanded the scope of options available to decision-makers, and the new options served to more closely align the interests of environmentalists and industry and thus helped to mitigate political opposition to CFC regulation. Evidence that showed the viability of alternatives thus was an asset for those seeking the phase out of CFCs. The development of substitutes changed the political dynamics of the ozone debate.

Because information is a resource in politics, opposing groups often use information to make arguments in support of particular policy alternatives. Such information is often but not always scientific. Scientific information is widely valued because of the high standing in which scientists are frequently held.[1] But in a world characterized by conflicts over values and flush with uncertainties, there exist powerful incentives to politicize information. Politicization occurs when those engaged in conflict evaluate policy alternatives according to the gains or losses they provide to a group's ability to bargain, negotiate, or compromise relative to its opponents.

This chapter provides a perspective on the debate on intervening in Iraq that took place in 2002 and early 2003. The debate over the Iraq war is meaningful in a book about science for two reasons. First, scientists might gain some perspective on the arguments presented here in a slightly unfamiliar, but closely related context. Indeed, intelligence in foreign policy plays the exact same role in a decision process as science in environmental policy (or health policy, energy policy, etc.). Fulton T. Armstrong, an analyst for the Central Intelligence Agency (CIA) has written of the role of intelligence analysis:

> The policymaker (or his or her boss) was elected by the American people to make value judgments. It is our job to develop a framework to help policymakers weigh multiple options, but their job to determine how to react to challenging situations, from turning the other cheek to staging a full confrontation . . . Our products should reflect an awareness of the immutable "national interests" as well as the range of policy options and political preferences – and not prejudge them for the policymaker.[2] (Armstrong 2002)

This conception of the role of the analyst is largely consistent with the notion of Honest Broker of Policy Alternatives.[3] This view is also consistent with well-developed theories about the different roles of information in the policy-making process.

> The *intelligence division* is the subgroup making available to the leadership facts and analyses, and clarifying goals and alternatives. It provides expectations, that is, for the consideration of the policy-makers of the group. The intelligence function may be distinguished from the *advisory function*, which recommends policy rather than merely presenting policy considerations. . . (Lasswell and Kaplan 1950: 193)

The role of information in decision-making is quite similar whether it is military intelligence or science-based intelligence.

A second reason why the role of intelligence in the Iraq war decision is worth considering is that the context of that decision was much more akin to contemporary situations of science in policy and politics than the national security decisions typical of the Cold War. The Cold War was characterized by a general agreement on goals, which were crystallized in the 1940s as containment of the Soviet Union. There was little uncertainty about the nature of the threat, as the Soviet Union had nuclear weapons and they were aimed at the United States. Intelligence in the Cold War was thus provided in a context where understandings of national interests and the nature of the threat were broadly shared and the role of intelligence was generally to be the arbiter of information. This was not the case in the context of the decision to go to war in Iraq, where the intelligence infrastructure was co-opted in support of advocating a single, desired political outcome – intelligence became stealth issue advocacy.

The debate leading to the war in Iraq and the role that information played in that debate provide a cautionary set of experiences for the scientific community. The Iraq case shows that information can indeed be used to advocate the case for a particular course of action, but if that information is presented, intentionally or not, to advance a predetermined political agenda, it may damage the credibility of the information providers and those who rely on information to argue for particular courses of action. In short, if you act as an Issue Advocate in the presentation of information but present yourself as anything but, it is extremely difficult to later seek to serve in any other role than as an Issue Advocate.

Iraq provided a first opportunity for the invocation of President George W. Bush's new geopolitical strategy of preemption. With preemption, President Bush wanted to change from the long-standing practice of inaction under conditions of an uncertain threat until that threat becomes imminent, to a default decision of action even if the threat is not imminent. President Bush upset a long-standing consensus on the role of military force in the service of national interests and thus added uncertainty about the goals of US foreign policy to debate about how that policy ought to be pursued. This made the Iraq war decision context much more similar to situations where we find contested science, such as the regulation of chemicals, adoption of the Kyoto Protocol on climate change, use of genetically modified crops and so on, because it was grounded in a debate over competing perspectives on risk and action in the face of uncertainty.

Lacking a consensus on preemption (i.e., a consensus on values, in the terminology of Chapter 4) as a guide to decisions in situations of uncertainty, the Bush Administration sought to build consensus on intervention in Iraq not as the specific application of a generally accepted principle (i.e., as a matter of Abortion Politics), but rather, based on the merits of the particular case, i.e., the dangers Iraq presented to the United States and its common interests (i.e., Tornado Politics). The Administration's commitment to preemption suggests that its decision-makers had come to agree that intervention in Iraq was its preferred policy alternative.[4] If so, then it makes sense that in making the case for intervention in Iraq the Administration had strong incentives to portray intelligence in a manner that supported its preferred policy over any alternatives.

The use of intelligence leading to the decision by the Bush Administration to intervene in Iraq exhibits dynamics that are not at all unique to this issue. It has much in common with the use of information by supporters of the so-called "precautionary principle" that is used to advocate action on environmental issues. The precautionary principle posits that uncertainty should not stand in the way of regulating actions potentially harmful to the environment. So, for example, under the precautionary principle some countries in Europe have temporarily banned genetically modified food because its long-term impacts on people or the environment are unknown – it is, they believe, better to be safe than sorry. The close similarity between the precautionary principle and preemption is notable because most supporters of each approach to decision-making come from points far removed on the ideological spectrum. That is, you will likely encounter very few people who support both President Bush's notion of preemption and Europe's notion of the precautionary principle in environmental policy.

How the doctrine of preemption encouraged the politicization of information

"Strategic doctrine" refers to the overarching policy framework that, in large degree, guides the foreign and domestic policies of the United States as they relate to its allies, enemies, and others worldwide. This framework has implications not only for the nation's military policies, but also its economic, social, humanitarian, and science and technology policies. Without question, President Bush's proposed doctrine of "preemption" not only represented a dramatic change in the strategic doctrine of the United States, but it also set the stage for a pathological politicization of intelligence.

The United States prospered for more than four decades during the Cold War under the strategic doctrine of "containment" and "deterrence" that was focused on limiting the global expansion of the Soviet Union. The Cold War policy of "containment" was first described in a 1947 article in *The Atlantic Monthly* by George Kennan, in which he wrote "it is clear that the main element of any United States policy toward the Soviet Union must be that of long-term, patient but firm and vigilant containment of Russian expansive tendencies" (Kennan 1947).

Although Kennan's proposed containment policy referred to political and military containment, the Cold War was fought through an arms race and regional conflict around the world, most notably in Korea and Vietnam, but in many other locations as well. In 1950, motivated by the Soviet Union's detonation of an atomic bomb, a National Security Council directive (NSC-68) characterized why containment required military superiority, "Without superior aggregate military strength, in being readily mobilizable, a policy of 'containment' – which is in effect a policy of calculated and gradual coercion – is no more than a policy of bluff" (US Department of State 1950).[5] This logic dictated that containment and deterrence required an ever-escalating arms race to succeed.

With the end of the Cold War, the administration of Bill Clinton proposed that "containment" and "deterrence" should give way to a policy of "enlargement" focused on managing the consequences of the globalization of international economies. In 1993, Anthony Lake, assistant to President Clinton for National Security Affairs, proposed that in the post-Cold War era "the successor to a doctrine of containment must be a strategy of enlargement – enlargement of the world's free community of market democracies" (Lake 1993).[6] Enlargement, according to Lake, had four components: the strengthening of developed market democracies, nurturing of new market democracies, liberalization of states hostile to market democracy, and advancing a humanitarian agenda.

For all practical purposes, September 11, 2001 marked the end of "enlargement" as the United States' post-Cold War strategic doctrine. In a speech in June 2002 at West Point, President Bush justified the need for a new strategic doctrine. He said:

> For much of the last century, America's defense relied on the Cold War doctrines of deterrence and containment. In some cases, those strategies still apply. But new threats also require new thinking. Deterrence – the promise of massive retaliation against nations – means nothing against shadowy terrorist networks with no nation or citizens to defend. Containment is not possible when unbalanced dictators with weapons of mass destruction can deliver those weapons on missiles or secretly provide them to terrorist allies. We cannot defend America and our friends by hoping for the best. We cannot put our faith in the word of tyrants, who solemnly sign non-proliferation treaties, and then systemically break them. If we wait for threats to fully materialize, we will have waited too long. (Bush 2002a)

In other words, uncertainty about threats could no longer be used as a justification for military inaction.

Thus, in the fall of 2002, the Bush Administration proposed "preemption" as a new approach to foreign policy. The concept of "preemption" is not new. The Department of Defense defines a "preemptive attack" as one "initiated on the basis of incontrovertible evidence that an enemy attack is imminent" (US Department of Defense 2001: 419). But President Bush envisioned a new kind of preemption, one that reflects a need "to adapt the concept of imminent threat to the capabilities and objectives of today's adversaries" (White House 2002: 15).[7] The Bush Administration sought to redefine preemption consistent with what the Department of Defense had traditionally called "preventative war . . . initiated in the belief that military conflict, while not imminent, is inevitable, and that to delay would involve greater risk" (US Department of Defense 2001: 423). The Bush Administration described its new policy of preemption consistent with the traditional notion of preventative war: "The greater the threat, the greater the risk of inaction – and the more compelling the case for taking anticipatory action to defend ourselves, even if uncertainty remains as to the time and place of the enemy's attack" (White House 2002: 15).

Preemption is thus a strategy for making decisions under circumstances of uncertainty. President Bush described preemption in September 2002 when he announced the "National Security Strategy of the United States," observing, "The gravest danger our Nation faces lies at the crossroads of radicalism and technology . . . And, as a matter of common sense and self-defense, America will act against such emerging threats before they are fully formed" (White House 2002: Introduction Letter, p. 2). The strategic doctrine proposed by President Bush had a broader intellectual basis. The US Commission on National Security of the Council on Foreign Relations, led by former Senators Gary Hart and Warren Rudman, argued in 2002 that the world had changed after September 11, 2001. They wrote that in the aftermath of September 11, "A proactive mindset is key . . . a reactive mindset is inevitably wasteful in terms of resources and can distract agencies from anticipating more probable future scenarios and undertaking protective measures" (Hart and Rudman 2002: 10). President George W. Bush agreed on the need for a proactive mindset. In his June 2002 speech President Bush said, "We must take the battle to the enemy, disrupt his plans, and confront the worst threats before they emerge. In the world we have entered, the only path to safety is the path of action. And this nation will act" (Bush 2002a).

Diverse values and ample uncertainty

As strategic doctrine, preemption makes a lot of sense when knowledge is certain and there is little political controversy, or in other words in the most simple of decision contexts described in Chapter 3. Examples of preemptive successes – among many – are vaccinations, which preempt disease; earthquake engineering, which preempts property damage and loss of life; and even government pensions, which preempt poverty among senior citizens. Each of these successes is based on certain knowledge and an overwhelming political consensus. The most effective roles for intelligence in such situations is typically equivalent to that of the Pure Scientist (i.e., keep your eyes out for risks) and Science Arbiter (e.g., does Iraq have weapons of mass destruction?).

By contrast, preemption has little hope for success when knowledge is uncertain and/or there is intense political conflict. In cases like the decision to go to war in Iraq, decisions must be made when the most honest statement about intelligence, scientific or otherwise, is simply, "We don't know for sure." This explains both the appeal of and need for strategies for decision-making under uncertainty. Under the Cold War's strategic doctrine of containment and deterrence there was arguably greater agreement on ends (i.e., the substance of the strategic doctrine) and there was less uncertainty about the nature of the threat – decades of the Cold War had helped to characterize clearly who the enemy was and its intentions.

But when political conflict over what to do occurs under conditions of intense conflict over values (what ends should be sought? with what means?) and information itself is highly uncertain (how large a threat is faced?), then these conditions create powerful incentives to politicize information in favor of a predetermined course of action. That is, these conditions create incentives for information providers to serve as Stealth Issue Advocates.

The Bush Administration's advocacy of a strategic doctrine of preemption was problematic because there was no political consensus, either nationally or internationally, on preemption as strategic doctrine. Consequently, the pursuit of a preemptive policy created incentives for the abuse and misuse of information. The debate over invading Iraq began not as a debate over Iraq but through the presentation of the doctrine of preemption by the Bush Administration.

In his State of the Union address in January 2003, President Bush presented the general case for preemption:

> Some have said we must not act until the threat is imminent. Since when have terrorists and tyrants announced their intentions, politely putting us on notice before they strike? If this threat is permitted to fully and suddenly emerge, all actions, all words, and all recriminations would come too late. Trusting in the sanity and restraint of Saddam Hussein is not a strategy, and it is not an option. (Bush 2003)

This perspective on decision-making under uncertainty is contrary to Article 51 of the United Nations Charter which states that there is an "inherent right of individual or collective self-defense if an armed attack occurs against a Member of the United Nations" (United Nations Charter 2006). Another interpretation of Article 51 is that in international relations nations are "innocent until proven guilty." In other words, the default position under conditions of an uncertain threat is that it is impermissible to launch an attack on another country. In response to the differences between preemption and Article 51, United Nations Secretary-General Kofi Annan remarked on September 23, 2003 that preemption "represents a fundamental challenge to the principles on which, however imperfectly, world peace and stability have rested for the last fifty-eight years" (CNN 2003).

Within the United States there is also a long history of opposition to preemption. Arthur Schlesinger, Jr., a historian, observes that Harry Truman, Dwight Eisenhower, and John F. Kennedy were opposed to such a doctrine. Truman rebuked a secretary of the Navy for calling for a preemptive war on the Soviet Union. Truman wrote in his memoirs, "I have always been opposed even to the thought of such a war. There is nothing more foolish than to think that war can be stopped by war. You don't 'prevent' anything except peace" (Schlesinger 2003).

And within the Bush Administration itself there apparently was disagreement on what preemption actually meant in practice.

According to the ubiquitous "senior administration official," the Bush Administration "never said that it was going to go around preempting in every circumstance . . . When we discussed the policy, we talked about the fact that it would be rare as an option" (Dobbs 2003). US citizens, as well as citizens around the world, did not accept preemption as a strategic doctrine when the war in Iraq was initiated. A CBS News poll taken of Americans in April 2003 after military action had begun in Iraq, found that overall only 42 percent of Americans supported preemption as strategic doctrine, and among those who supported the intervention in Iraq, only half supported preemption (CBS News 2003).

In a situation where there was no general agreement on the doctrine of preemption, i.e., what to do under conditions of uncertainty, the Bush Administration turned to arguing the merits of intervention in Iraq. It presented intelligence in the form of Science Arbiter but was in fact acting as Issue Advocate. Instead of a war of necessity – which would have been necessary under a generally accepted doctrine of preemption – the Bush Administration characterized the war in Iraq as a war of choice. President Bush based his advocacy on certainty in information on the nature of the Iraqi threat, some of it scientific, such as the aluminum tubes ostensibly imported by Iraq for a nuclear program, that suggest that Iraq posed a direct threat to the United States and its interests.

For example, in September 2002, before the United Nations General Assembly, President Bush made the following claims:

> The history, the logic, and the facts lead to one conclusion: Saddam Hussein's regime is a grave and gathering danger. To suggest otherwise is to hope against the evidence. To assume this regime's good faith is to bet the lives of millions and the peace of the world in a reckless gamble. And this is a risk we must not take.

> Delegates to the General Assembly, we have been more than patient. We've tried sanctions. We've tried the carrot of oil for food,

and the stick of coalition military strikes. But Saddam Hussein has defied all these efforts and continues to develop weapons of mass destruction. The first time we may be completely certain he has nuclear weapons is when, God forbid, he uses one. We owe it to all our citizens to do everything in our power to prevent that day from coming. (Bush 2002b)

And in February 2003, Secretary of State Colin Powell made the following statement before the United Nations:

The facts and Iraq's behavior show that Saddam Hussein and his regime are concealing their efforts to produce more weapons of mass destruction . . . There can be no doubt that Saddam Hussein has biological weapons and the capability to rapidly produce more, many more. And he has the ability to dispense these lethal poisons and diseases in ways that can cause massive death and destruction . . . Saddam Hussein has chemical weapons. (Powell 2003)

Aided by hindsight (see Gellman and Pincus 2003; Preist and Pincus 2003), what is problematic about these sorts of claims made by advocates of intervention in Iraq is captured in a statement by Robin Cook, a member of Tony Blair's Cabinet who resigned his position in March 2003 in protest over Iraq. He said "Instead of using intelligence as evidence on which to base a decision about policy, we used intelligence as the basis on which to justify a policy on which we had already settled" (Hoge 2003). Intelligence became a servant of stealth issue advocacy, rather than a resource supporting the information needs of decision-makers, helping to characterize risks, uncertainties, and options.

The politics of preemption were such that absent agreement on the general values of strategic doctrine, debate supposedly about intelligence was really a mask for an underlying debate about values. As so often is the case, a debate more accurately characterized as Abortion Politics was presented as a matter of Tornado Politics. Information then became an asset to be used to achieve victory in the debate over values, rather than a source of enlightenment. For the Bush Administration, this meant that, as E. J. Dionne wrote in *The Washington Post*, "The president used the tactics of a political campaign to sell the war in Iraq" (Dionne 2003). Intelligence that might have suggested policy options other than a quick invasion was deemphasized in favor of information that supported a particular course of action. Intelligence was treated as a tool of issue advocacy, and certainly not as a component of the Honest Brokering of Policy Alternatives.

A number of Bush Administration officials, including Donald Rumsfeld, Paul Wolfowitz, Dick Cheney, Richard Armitage, Douglas Feith, and Lewis Libby, were on record long before September 11, 2001 about their desire to remove Saddam Hussein from power (Weisman 2003). There is thus no need for some grand conspiracy theory to argue that in the context of (a) lack of consensus on preemption, and (b) uncertainty about the imminence of a threat, preemption as a strategic doctrine encouraged the use of information to justify a course of action already determined to be a desired outcome of political debate over Iraq. The Bush Administration used information like an Issue Advocate seeking to carefully select and shape information that best supported the political agenda that it had already decided on (Gellman and Pincus 2003).

According to Arthur Schlesinger, Jr. the conflict between stealth issue advocacy and intelligence gathering was well understood by a young Abraham Lincoln, who in 1848 wrote a letter to his law partner with opinions on the US–Mexican war:

> Allow the President to invade a neighboring nation whenever he shall deem it necessary to repel an invasion and you allow him to do so whenever he may choose to say he deems it necessary for such purpose, and you allow him to make war at pleasure . . . If today he should say he thinks it necessary to invade Canada to prevent the British from invading us, how could you stop him? You might say to him, "I see no

probability of the British invading us," but he will say to you, "Be silent: I see it if you don't." (Schlesinger 2003)

The end of preemption?

Some might claim that there is nothing particularly special about the Iraq case. That is, in *any* situation characterized by value conflict and inherent uncertainty there are strong incentives for the politicization of information – deciding a course of action and then finding information to support it is common across the political spectrum. And this is indeed my general point. The politics of preemption and the Iraq war are characteristic of the trend in contemporary politics to wage value disputes through information. This is problematic if information about different policy options really does matter in decision-making. One way in which people will make such judgments about the importance of information is to draw on some conception of what democracy is supposed to look like. A view that emphasizes interest group pluralism (as discussed in Chapter 2) will find less wrong with the Bush administration's approach to the Iraq war than a view more consistent with E. E. Schattschneider's realist conception of democracy as a debate over options.

Whatever one's views on the appropriateness of the Bush Administration's tactics leading to invading Iraq, or the war itself, it seems clear that the Bush Administration's approach to justifying the war handicapped its subsequent ability to make similar decisions by discrediting its own intelligence agencies. If hindsight showed that the intelligence on which the Bush Administration based its decision to go to war in Iraq was flawed (which it has), then the Bush administration would be criticized (which it has been) for playing fast and loose with intelligence to compel its favored political outcome. In subsequent situations any claims by the Bush Administration about imminent risks would be rightly viewed with a skeptical eye, regardless of the reality of those risks.

Thus, in a failed effort to avoid lost credibility in 2003 the Bush administration made efforts to recast the decision to go to war in Iraq as a necessary decision under the doctrine of preemption, and not a war of choice compelled by intelligence. Consider the following three examples of attempts to reframe the decision to go to war as motivated not by information, but by general principles of decision-making under uncertainty.

First, when asked in a public forum in the summer of 2003 whether the apparent non-existence of weapons of mass destruction meant that government intelligence agencies had messed up, Deputy Defense Secretary Paul Wolfowitz replied that "Being wrong in this business does not mean messing up" (Schmitt 2003). And under a doctrine of preemption the statement by Secretary Wolfowitz is exactly right. Uncertainty means "we don't know" and that even best guesses can be wrong. In this case uncertainty referred to the presence of WMDs in Iraq. Under preemption, uncertainty is not a reason for inaction, nor presumably is being wrong. Preemption provides guidance in such situations of uncertainty: err on the side of eliminating the risk. Better safe than sorry.

Second, consider another statement, this one made by Defense Secretary Donald Rumsfeld in July, several months after the US intervention in Iraq began, "The coalition did not act in Iraq because we had discovered dramatic new evidence of Iraq's pursuit of weapons of mass murder. We acted because we saw the existing evidence in a new light, through the prism of our experience on September 11" (Risen et al. 2003). In other words, according to Rumsfeld the United States did not act because of information, but because it had adopted a new strategic doctrine of preemption. Rumsfeld's statement reflects an appeal to Abortion Politics in the face of a clear failure in the Tornado Politics that the Administration relied on to sell the war to the American public. Contrary to Secretary Rumsfeld's assertion, information about the immediacy of the threat posed by Iraq to the United States and its neighbors was a key element in justifying the war. There was in fact no values consensus on preemption.

Third, British Prime Minister Tony Blair spoke before the US Congress in July 2003, of the decision to go to war in Iraq, in terms of uncertainty and preemption, and not as a war of choice:

> Can we be sure that terrorism and weapons of mass destruction will join together? Let us say one thing: If we are wrong, we will have destroyed a threat that at its least is responsible for inhuman carnage and suffering. That is something I am confident history will forgive. But if our critics are wrong, if we are right, as I believe with every fiber of instinct and conviction I have that we are, and we do not act, then we will have hesitated in the face of this menace when we should have given leadership. That is something history will not forgive. But precisely because the threat is new, it isn't obvious. It turns upside-down our concepts of how we should act and when, and it crosses the frontiers of many nations. So just as it redefines our notions of security, so it must refine our notions of diplomacy. (Blair 2003)

Each of these examples illustrates how advocates for war in Iraq began with an argument based on the value of preemption, but found the politics to be unfavorable to reaching a consensus. The Bush administration thus switched political strategies to an approach much more consistent with Tornado Politics, arguing that information compelled a particular action. When the action was ultimately taken to invade Iraq, then the Iraq war advocates sought to again reframe the action a second time, this time again in terms of the dynamics of Abortion Politics, to suggest that a consensus on values had been achieved, when, in fact, they had not. Dressing up an issue that is fundamentally Abortion Politics in the guise of Tornado Politics created incentives for the Bush Administration's misuse of intelligence in political advocacy in support of the Iraq war.[8]

One lesson of the role of intelligence in the selling of the Iraq war is that the Bush Administration may have ended all chances for its proposed doctrine of preemption to take hold. In other words, by seeking to justify the war based on intelligence that it argued showed a pending threat, the Bush Administration successfully sold to the public a war in Iraq, but in the process it lost any chance of reaching a consensus on the need to adopt a new strategic doctrine grounded in the notion of preemption (*New York Times* 2004). In short, the Bush Administration tried to have it both ways – it wanted to justify the war in Iraq as the first invocation of a new doctrine of preemption as preventative war, but it also wanted to appeal to the old definition of preemption as intervention based on incontrovertible evidence of a threat. For the Bush Administration this schizophrenic strategy successfully sold the war but failed to sell the new doctrine of preemption, and with it any hopes of fundamentally changing US strategic doctrine.

The Bush Administration's protean approach to selling the war has led to confusion about why we went to war in the first place. For example, Senator Jay Rockefeller (D-WV) stated, "We did not go to war to bring democracy and prosperity and peace to Iraq . . . It was all about weapons of mass destruction and the imminent threat of America getting attacked" (Mann 2003). In stark contrast, Secretary of Defense Donald Rumsfeld explained, "The coalition did not act in Iraq because we had discovered dramatic new evidence of Iraq's pursuit of weapons of mass murder" (NewsHour 2003). Did the United States go to war because it changed how it viewed the notion of imminent threat or because Iraq posed an imminent threat, as always understood? The answer is "Yes, for both reasons."

Lack of resolution on the notion of preemption is significant because in the aftermath of September 11, 2001 how decisions are made in the face of uncertain threats is *the* key question of US national security. But the decision to go to war in Iraq will provide little guidance on how to make future national security decisions under conditions of uncertainty. So for many United States citizens, and their elected representatives, preemption still means what it always has meant – military action and accountability for past actions are decided case-by-case based on what evidence is known through intelligence about the magnitude and imminence of particular threats.

Politics is all about reducing choices to a single preferred course of action – e.g., go to war in Iraq, yes or no? For politics to do its job there must first be alternatives. But when the desired course of action is already decided upon, then alternatives are not needed. In such circumstances intelligence becomes a tool in the quest for political victory on the predetermined option. And one way that political victory can be achieved is by leaving no room for choice.

The quest for certainty required by a commitment to preemption elevated the role of politics in policy and diminished the actual role of information and intelligence. It transformed intelligence into a form of advocacy. In situations of profound uncertainty or irreconcilable differences in values, flexible or robust policies that evolve based on public participation and the lessons of experience may make more sense than large-scale commitments where there is little chance to correct mistakes. The motivations of political advocates who seek large changes may help to explain the turn to preemption in situations of uncertainty and political conflict.

Bad outcomes are all but guaranteed when all policy alternatives before decision-makers are bad ones. For instance, the debate over the war on Iraq may have been misguided, as better policy options than "war: yes or no?" may have been ignored. Such ignorance was apparently willful. The pathological politicization of intelligence served as a constraint on options that might have been more effective but, for certain ideologues, politically less desirable. The Bush Administration's approach to entering the Iraq war depended upon limiting the scope of choice by treating intelligence as a tool of issue advocacy rather than an Honest Brokering of Policy Alternatives. A lack of choice also threatens democracy because it elevates politics above policy, and it substitutes consideration of creative policy alternatives with political battle over predetermined positions.

There are many incentives that lure us into political battles where stealth issue advocacy tends to squeeze out Honest Brokering of Policy Alternatives. A first step toward care in using science, or information more generally, in politics is to understand those circumstances which encourage disputes over values to be mapped onto debates over science.

EIGHT

When scientists politicize science

It is characteristic of the science and politics of the early twenty-first century to see scientists actively engaged in political debates, and particularly as related to the environment. For example, when a 2003 paper in the journal *Climate Research* argued that twentieth-century climate variations were unexceptional in millenial perspective, advocacy groups opposed to the Kyoto Protocol predictably hailed the research as "sound science," while advocacy groups in support of the Protocol called the paper "junk science" (Regalado 2003). In this case, more troubling than the "cherry picking" of scientific results by Issue Advocates is that many scientists' evaluations of the *scientific merit* of the *Climate Research* paper correlated perfectly with their public expressions of support for or opposition to the Kyoto Protocol on climate change. Acceptance of the paper's conclusions was equated with opposition to Kyoto, and correspondingly, rejection of the paper's findings was equated with support for Kyoto. For example, one prominent climate scientist (on record as supporting Kyoto) suggested in testimony before the US Congress that the paper must be bad science because the editor who oversaw its publication had been critical of the Intergovernmental Panel on Climate Change and the Kyoto Protocol (Collins 2003). And the editor (a social scientist who is on record as opposing Kyoto) of a different journal that published a second version of the controversial paper commented, "I'm following my political agenda – a bit, anyway, but isn't that the right of the editor?" (Monastersky 2003).

If scientists evaluate the research findings of their peers on the basis of the implications for issue advocacy, then "scientific" debate among academics risks morphing into political debates. From the perspective of the public or policy-makers, scientific debate and political debate on many environmental issues already have become indistinguishable, and such cases of conflation limit the role of science in the development of creative and feasible policy options. In many instances science has become little more than a mechanism for marketing competing political agendas, and scientists have become leading members of the advertising campaigns.

No recent example of this dynamic has received the amount of attention among the mainstream media as the controversy over *The Skeptical Environmentalist* (hereafter *TSE*) (Lomborg 2001a). Heated debate and controversy are rather the norm insofar as environmental issues are concerned, but reaction to *TSE* spilled over from the environmental community on to the pages of leading newspapers and magazines around the world, and has thus come to occupy the attention of scholars who study science in its broader societal setting.

Why does the politicization of science among scientists matter? Consider the following controversy over science, policy, and politics. In October 2002 a number of scientists expressed concern that President Bush appeared to be "stacking" health advisory panels with scientists chosen more for their political views than their scientific credentials. A group of scientists writing in *Science* explained that,

> instead of grappling with scientific ambiguity and shaping public policy using the best available evidence (the fundamental principle underlying public health and environmental regulation), we can now expect these committees to emphasize the uncertainties of health and environmental risks, supporting the administration's antiregulatory

views. And in those areas where there are deeply held conflicts in values, we can expect only silence. (Michaels *et al.* 2002)

In other words, rather than seeking to understand the significance of science in the context of specific policy alternatives, these committees would instead be serving as Issue Advocates and correspondingly focus on the political challenge of bolstering support for decisions already made, presumably based on factors other than science, such as ideology. Few would disagree with the premise that scientific outcomes should not be predetermined by political perspectives. Why? The result, invariably, would be bad science and most likely bad policy. But what about reversing the direction of causality? Do scientific perspectives determine political outcomes, as suggested by the linear model?

This chapter argues that in the case of *TSE* many scientists acted as if science does in fact compel certain political outcomes under the framework of the linear model. In other words, scientists framed debate over *TSE* as a matter of Tornado Politics under an expectation that getting the facts straight would necessarily compel a certain response. In fact, debate over *TSE* has had more in common with Abortion Politics, with scientists taking on the role of Issue Advocates (sometimes overtly, but often in stealth fashion). Almost completely absent from the debate was any scientist or scientific organization taking on the role of Honest Broker of Policy Alternatives. Examples of similar situations abound in areas as diverse as international whaling (Aron *et al.* 2002), cloning (Nature Publishing Group 2002), sex education (Clymer 2002), the history of firearms (Postel 2002), and North American archeology (Custred 2002), to list just a very few. The debate that followed publication of *TSE* (and continues to reverberate in debates about the environment, seemingly without end), saw an unprecedented mobilization of not just environmental groups but many scientists, against the book, its author, and its publisher.

Of course, a focus on the intersection of politics and science is not new; it has been studied for decades.[1] The science and technology studies community has developed considerable expertise in and understanding of the broader social and political context of science, including the causes and consequences of the politicization of science in political settings (Jasanoff 1987; Jasanoff and Wynne 1998; Kitcher 2001; Rayner 2003; Sarewitz 1996). The politicization of science by scientists themselves is a topic that by contrast has received somewhat less attention than the politicization of science by politicians and Issue Advocates.[2] What may be new, or at least more meaningful than in the past, is the degree to which scientists themselves encourage political conflict through science (Starobin 2006).

Controversy over *The Skeptical Environmentalist*: political battle not policy debate

In *TSE* Bjørn Lomborg, a Danish statistician by training and a self-described environmentalist, advances a view popularized by the late Julian Simon, an economist, that environmental problems are not as severe as advertised by environmental groups, and that some combination of business-as-usual and incremental change will be sufficient for children born today to "get more food, a better education, a higher standard of living, more leisure time and far more possibilities – without the global environment being destroyed" (Lomborg 2001a: 352).[3] Reaction to the book, published by Cambridge University Press. was both quick and diverse. *The Economist* (2001) wrote "This is one of the most valuable books on public policy – not merely on environmental policy – to have been written for the intelligent reader in the past ten years." *Rolling Stone* (Goodell 2001) gave a similarly positive review, "Lomborg pulls off the remarkable feat of welding the techno-optimism of the Internet age with a lefty's concern for the fate of the planet." In contrast, *Scientific American* (Rennie 2002) wrote,

"The book is a failure," and *Grist Magazine* (Schultz 2001) concluded "The Skeptical Environmentalist is C-minus stuff, as straightforward and lackluster as a 10th-grade term paper."

Especially in light of its favorable reception in some quarters, for many environmental advocates *TSE* must have seemed like a declaration of war. Environmental groups such as the World Resources Institute and Union of Concerned Scientists began an aggressive public campaign seeking to discredit Lomborg and Cambridge University Press (see, e.g., Union of Concerned Scientists 2003; World Resources Institute 2001). A representative of the Union of Concerned Scientists justified the offensive as a preemptive political strategy: "this book is going to be misused terribly by interests opposed to a clean energy policy" (Woodard 2001). It is not a surprise to see an organized campaign among environmental advocacy groups to advance their own causes by discrediting the book, or (although to a lesser degree) organized support of *TSE* by economic interests who favor the book's message. As self-identified special interests it is the job of these groups to push their agenda using whatever strategies may be effective. The attention with which *TSE* was greeted provided a convenient resource for advocates to hitch their agendas to – using *TSE* in both positive and negative fashion.[4]

In this context a number of respected scientists saw fit to enter the political fray over *TSE*, and largely in support of environmental advocates. It would be easy to dismiss the politicization of science by scientists as the province of industry-supported scientists-*cum*-consultants whose credentials support their "hired-gun" role in issue advocacy. But the case of *TSE* shows this caricature to be too simplistic.

That some scientists engage in political activities is neither new nor problematic; they are after all citizens. A problem exists when, in the case of their opposition to *TSE*, scientists implicitly or explicitly equate scientific arguments with political arguments, and in the process reinforce a simplistic and misleading view of how science supports policy. As argued in previous chapters, the logic of the linear model encouraged stealth issue advocacy and deemphasized the honest brokering of policy alternatives. In the process of couching advocacy in science, scientists risk damaging the potentially positive contributions of their own special expertise to effective decision-making. Scientists seeking political victories through science may find this strategy expedient in the short term, but over the long run it may diminish the constructive role that scientific expertise can play in the policy process. As we saw in the case of the debate leading to the Iraq war, the ability to use knowledge as a resource in decision-making may be compromised when there is a conflation of Tornado Politics (i.e., shared values, low uncertainty in knowledge) with Abortion Politics (i.e., lack of shared values, knowledge ambiguous or irrelevant).

It is crucial to observe that with very few exceptions the debate over *TSE* focused not on specific policy alternatives, but instead on the overarching political implications putatively compelled by *TSE*. In other words, the debate over *TSE* focused on the advantages or disadvantages the book putatively lent to opposing political perspectives, with only a rare nod toward the particular policy recommendations associated with those perspectives. The absence of policy debate related to *TSE* is troubling because science alone cannot determine who wins and who loses in political battles (Jasanoff and Wynne 1998).[5]

In the case of *TSE*, scientists served as Stealth Issue Advocates when they claimed that Lomborg has gotten his "science" wrong, and because he has his science wrong then necessarily those who accept his views of "science" should lose out in political battle. Such stealth issue advocacy is problematic if scientific proof is "overrated" in political debate (Oreskes 2004), or if science in fact makes environmental controversies more intractable (Sarewitz 2004). At a minimum, this sort of politicization of science by scientists runs contrary to understandings held by the science and technology studies community about the nuanced, protean, and complex interface of science and decision-making, in which science is "co-produced" by various sectors of society, and separation of "facts" and "values" cannot be achieved (e.g., Jasanoff 1990).

Some scientists in opposition to Lomborg lent their credibility and stature to interest groups who then used the authority of the scientists as the basis for making a political claim. At the request of the Union of Concerned Scientists (UCS) these scientists prepared essays critical of several of Lomborg's claims but which avoided any explicit discussion of politics or policy. The UCS then justified their engagement of scientists against Lomborg in explicitly political terms: "groups with anti-environmental agendas use these works to promote their objectives . . . Like the Hare, Lomborg's lie has raced out in front of the truth. With the help of these careful scientific peer reviews, UCS hopes that the truth, like the Tortoise, will catch up and emerge the ultimate victor (Union of Concerned Scientists 2003)."[6] And it is clear in this instance that "truth" manifests itself not simply in knowledge, but in political victory.

Other scientists saw no need to cloak their agendas and were quite open about their political motivations for attacking *TSE*, making their role as Issue Advocates difficult to overlook. Consider the following three examples.

First, Peter Raven, the director of the Missouri Botanical Garden and president of the American Association for the Advancement of Science, joined with a number of colleagues to lobby Cambridge University Press, the book's publisher, to cease publication (Goldstein 2002). In response to a question about why he is focusing attention on *TSE*, Raven hints at policy but does not discuss specific alternatives, and instead expresses concern that the perspective presented in *TSE* might enhance the political power of those in opposition to his own political perspective?:

It either can be very expensive to change the bases of whole economies on fossil fuels to avoid global warming, which is something that makes governments extremely nervous and for very understandable reasons or, on the other hand, one can believe those who say that the development of alternative energy modes, hydrogen fuel, nuclear fusion, wind power and so forth will provide the basis of whole new industries and will end up enriching economies and making them better off in the not very distant future. Making the transition though is hugely disruptive, and I think it's against that background that one can understand that, if somebody comes along and says: aside from the moon being made of blue cheese there is really no environmental problem, everything is getting better, and a lot of people have said a lot of things over the years and some of them are not true and probably not true now and blah, blah, blah – they will be warmly received by those who wish to win exemptions from the need to do anything.[7]

Second, Stuart Pimm (2003), a professor of ecology at Duke University, justifies his opposition to *TSE* in terms of a metaphor, "when you are sick, please go to a professional physician and not a quack for help." Or in other words, who gets a voice in environmental controversies? Presumably, Pimm equates Lomborg with the "quack" and those scientists who share his views in opposition to Lomborg with the "physician." The patient is presumably the policy-maker looking to make a decision.

Third, the scientists who served on the Danish Committees on Scientific Dishonesty, which was convened to investigate allegations of scientific fraud in *TSE* made by environmental scientists critical of *TSE*, concluded that

the many, particularly American researchers, who have received Bjørn Lomborg's book with great gusto, even in a specifically negative fashion, are unlikely to have even given the book the time of day unless it had received such overwhelmingly positive write-ups in leading American newspapers and in *The Economist*. The USA is the society with the highest energy consumption in the world, and there are powerful interests in the USA bound up with increasing energy consumption and with the belief in free market forces. (Danish Committees on Scientific Dishonesty 2003: 10)

The placement of these various perspectives in the popular media and on the internet, rather than in technical journals, show very clearly that many of the scientists who vehemently criticized *TSE* and Cambridge University Press perceived the stakes to be not simply a battle over findings, methods, epistemology, or disciplines that often characterize scientific debates within the academic enterprise, or even conflicts among Science Arbiters disagreeing on positive questions posed by decision-makers. Instead, the debate initiated by scientists over *TSE* was about who should have authority and power to decide what sort of world we collectively wish to live in. The debate was about political power and scientists readily chose sides as Issue Advocates.[8]

The linear model and issue advocacy

The perspectives of those who have argued that because the science of *TSE* is wrong, a certain set of political views must also be wrong, reinforce, reflect, and derive from an ontological and epistemological view of the role of science in society that assumes that science can and should compel political outcomes. This is of course an invocation of the "linear model" (Chapter 6) because it is based on first getting the science "right" as a necessary, if not sufficient, basis for decision-making (cf., Oreskes 2004; Sarewitz 2004). Consequently, when scientists reinforce the linear model it has the potential to create pathologies in decision-making, and in particular the conflation of Abortion and Tornado Politics. As argued in Chapter 6, the linear model may be more effective at bringing politics into science than science into policy (see, e.g., Jasanoff 1987; Wynne 1991).

From the perspective of the linear model, science not only plays a (if not the) central role in political battle, but because scientific understandings are supposed to motivate political action, winning a scientific debate leads to a privileged position in political battle. Consequently, scientific debates *are* in effect political debates because resolving scientific debates will resolve political conflicts. Science thus becomes a convenient and necessary means for removing certain options from a debate without explicitly dealing with disputes over values. The linear model can seem like the Issue Advocate's trump card in political debates. For who can argue against truth?

A perfect example of the linear model in action can be found in debate over global climate change. Within this debate, studies that show meaningful connections between greenhouse gas emissions and actual or projected climate changes are interpreted as supportive of action to reduce emissions, and thus climate change as well, whereas studies that challenge the significance of such connections are interpreted as casting doubt on the need for such action (Pielke 2004c). Action is typically narrowly defined as the Kyoto Protocol and the political stakes are victory in either securing or denying its implementation. Under the linear model both sides argue about science as a proxy for actually discussing the worth and practicality of possible alternative courses of action, of which the Kyoto Protocol is but one of many. On the climate debate many assume that victory in debate on scientific issues, as perceived by the public, ought to compel victory in political debate. Hence we see arguments in the popular media and the internet over many individual studies that are released (notable examples of recent years include the temperature record of the past 1,000 years and surface versus tropospheric temperature trends). Missed in this enterprise are policy alternatives that are robust with respect to the scientific disagreements (Lempert 2000; Rayner and Malone 1998; Sarewitz and Pielke 2000). The linear model brings scientific debates to the fore as a prerequisite to other action, and encourages the mapping of political agendas onto scientific findings.

How scientists used the linear model in debate over TSE

In order to take advantage of the logic of the linear model, Lomborg's critics argued that his science was wrong, and therefore the politics (and crucially, not policies, because policies largely were not discussed in *TSE*, or by its critics) of those who accept his scientific arguments must also be wrong. This of course is the same logic that underlies frequent invocations of "junk science" and "sound science" in contemporary debates involving science (Herrick and Jamieson 2000). Under the linear model, invoking the phrase "junk science" means that one believes that political agendas following from that science must be ill conceived and not deserving of support. Invoking the phrase "sound science" means that one believes that political agendas following from that science are right, just, and deserving of support. Battles take place over whether science is sound or junk instead of debating the value or practicality of specific policy alternatives.

Followers of the linear model would likely argue that it really does matter for policy whether or not the information presented in *TSE* is "junk" or "sound" science. Two examples from *TSE* show why this line of argument cannot succeed. First, consider the issue of forests. On this issue, Lomborg and the World Resources Institute (WRI) and World Wildlife Fund (WWF) engaged in a lengthy debate over various scientific matters covered in *TSE*, as well as the credentials of Lomborg to even discuss forests.[9] Missing from this debate was the fact that of the forest policy alternatives mentioned in *TSE* most were simultaneously advocated also by WRI, WWF, or both (cf., Dower *et al.* 1997); among them: in developing countries, plant quick-growing trees to provide fuel, use cheap metal and ceramic stoves to increase efficiency and reduce indoor pollution, reduce poverty and increase growth, and in developed countries, pay developing countries for preservation, e.g., debt for nature swaps, increase plantations, institute a global certification system for green forest products (Lomborg 2001a: 114–117).[10] And none of the forest policy options discussed in *TSE* was objected to by WRI/WWF in their critique.

In this case a vigorous debate over science was completely irrelevant to the course of action recommended by either side of the debate, as they were both largely in agreement on policy options. Thus, from the perspective of action, it simply did not matter whether the scientific arguments of WRI/WWF or Lomborg were closer to the truth. The recommended actions were apparently robust to disagreements about the science of forests. Of course, from the perspective of politics the outcome of the scientific debate may determine who has a voice in forest policy-making and who does not. The WRI/WWF debate with Lomborg over forests was putatively about science, but it was really about politics.

Consider as well the issue of climate change. *TSE*'s chapter on climate change recognizes the authority of the Intergovernmental Panel on Climate Change as the leading body of expertise on climate science. But even with this acceptance Lomborg judged the Kyoto Protocol to be too expensive for the benefits that result. *TSE*'s critics (e.g., Schneider 2002) arrived at a different conclusion, and judged the Kyoto Protocol's benefits to exceed its costs. In this instance, evaluating *TSE*'s presentation of climate science as "junk" or "sound" is irrelevant to understanding the course of action recommended by either side because judgments of the value of costs versus benefits is a highly subjective, value-laden calculation. In this case Lomborg and his critics basically agree on the science – global warming is real, it will have impacts on people and the environment, and there will be more "losers" than "winners" from climate change – but differ a great deal on what the science signifies for action. Despite such general agreement on science, *TSE*'s critics focused on minor differences about the science in *TSE* rather than discussing broader issues of policy (e.g., Mahlman 2001). Again, from the perspective of politics, the outcome of this putatively scientific debate may determine who has a voice in climate policy-making and who does not.

Under the linear model, science supposedly dictates which policies make sense and which do not. But reality does not conform to the linear model, as shown from the examples of debate over forests and climate in *TSE*. Under the dynamics of Abortion Politics, disagreement about science does not preclude consensus on action, and general agreement about science does not preclude opposing views on action. But even in the face of ample evidence that the linear model cannot explain the relationship of science and policy (see, e.g., Oreskes 2004; Sarewitz 2004), it continues to shape discussion and debate on science-related issues, arguably because it is convenient for scientists who serve as Issue Advocates in political debate.

The linear model was the explicit basis for, or subtext of, many of the claims made by environmental scientists against *TSE*. Examples of various explicit and implicit invocations of the linear model include Thomas Lovejoy, of the World Bank, writing in *Scientific American* against *TSE*, explaining to Lomborg how the world actually works. "Researchers identify a potential problem. Scientific examination tests the various hypotheses, understanding of the problem often becomes more complex, researchers suggest remedial policies – then the situation improves" (Lovejoy 2002). In other words, science and scientists drive politics in a sequential, linear manner. Another vocal critic of *TSE*, John Holdren (2002), of Harvard, invoked the linear model when he explained his motivation for participating in an extensive series of critiques of *TSE* in the popular press. "If the issue involves science for policy, moreover, a clear and forceful denunciation has the further purpose of avoiding an extreme and poorly founded interpretation of the relevant science being credited in the policy debate as lying within the range of respectable scientific opinion" (2002).[11] But even as he invokes the notion of policy, Holdren does not discuss specific policies, and instead focuses on the role that science plays in politics for determining which sort of policies are acceptable and which are not. Holdren also justified his critique of *TSE* in terms of the Pure Scientist, "To expose this pastiche of errors and misrepresentations was not a political act but a scientific duty" (Holdren 2003). Under the linear model, it makes perfect sense to conduct scientific debates before the public and policy-makers because the linear model holds that getting the science "right" is necessary for effective policy-making to occur. Holdren writes:

> [Lomborg] has needlessly muddled public understanding and wasted immense amounts of the time of capable people who have had to take on the task of rebutting him. And he has done so at the particular intersection of science with public policy – environment and the human condition – where public and policy-maker confusion about the realities is more dangerous for the future of society than on any other science-and-policy question excepting, possibly, the dangers from weapons of mass destruction. (Holdren 2002)

But if the linear model fails to accurately represent the relationship of science and decision-making, then following it in practice serves mainly to enhance the pathological politicization of science.

Scientific American's framing of its January 2002 collection of critical responses to Lomborg by scientists and environmentalists is also an invocation of the linear model. The essays were published with the subtitle invoking the notion of the Pure Scientist, "Science defends itself against *The Skeptical Environmentalist*" (Rennie 2002), as if Lomborg's critics were speaking for science itself. Again, this makes perfect sense under an expectation that science dictates political outcomes. From this perspective, because particular scientific results compel certain actions and not others, there is little reason to distinguish science from politics. Consequently, the following subtitle would thus have been synonymous, "Our political perspective defends itself against the political agenda of *The Skeptical Environmentalist*" but it would have carried with it far less authority than masking politics in the cloth of science.

Lomborg himself appears to accept the linear model when he writes in *TSE*, "Getting the state of the world right is important because it defines humanity's problems and shows us where our actions are most needed" (Lomborg 2001a: 3). Lomborg further writes, "indeed, there is no other basis for sound political decisions than the best available scientific evidence" (2001a: 5). And,

> thus, with this assessment of the state of the world I wish to leave to the individual reader the political judgment as to where we should focus our efforts. Instead, it is my intention to provide the best possible information about how things have progressed and are likely to develop in the future, so that the democratic process is assured the soundest basis for decisions. (2001a: 6)

For those who accept the linear model, Lomborg could not be any more provocative. For those who reject the linear model, Lomborg may seem to be less threatening as another member of a large set of people and groups from across the political spectrum seeking to advance their agendas selectively using science to make the best possible case in support of their arguments (Funtowicz and Ravetz 1992; Herrick and Jamieson 2000; Wynne 1991). This may help to explain why some scientists reacted to TSE with venom while others who may also have differed with Lomborg's politics reacted with indifference. [12]

A reviewer of an earlier draft of this chapter noted that the ample policy credentials of many of the critical scientist-advocates indicate that their invocation of the linear model must have been more a matter of political calculus than adherence to a misleading worldview. This may or may not be the case; but my argument does not depend upon discerning the motivations behind those scientists who use science to further their political agendas. The consequences of invoking and following a linear model are significant in either case.

Students of science and society might object to this line of argument by noting that because the linear model has been largely discredited as a descriptive and normative theory of the relation of science with the rest of society (e.g., Guston and Kensiton 1994; Kitcher 2001; Sarewitz 1996; Stokes 1997), its plausibility as a practical framework within which to wage political battle might be called into question. But despite its critics, within the scientific community, the linear model remains a widely held perspective on how science does and should connect with the rest of society (e.g., Greenberg 2001; Sarewitz 1996). My experience in working closely with scientists for close to twenty years suggests that despite robust STS research to the contrary, many practicing scientists are blissfully unaware of the critiques of the linear model of science that so many continue to believe in. To the extent that this characterization faithfully describes many practicing scientists, it represents a failure of the science studies community to share their knowledge with those to whom it matters most. Moreover, independent of intellectual understandings of the complexity of relationships between science and politics, there are powerful incentives for its adherents to invoke the linear model, because action based on the linear model confers mutually reinforcing benefits among scientists, politicians, and interest groups (Pielke 2002).

Lessons of the debate over *TSE*

The linear model also helps to explain why *TSE* received such a vitriolic response from some members of the scientific community as compared to books with a similar thesis, such as works by Gregg Easterbrook (1995), Ronald Bailey (1993), and Julian Simon (1996). One biologist suggested that Easterbrook and Simon could be easily dismissed because they are not environmental scientists, "Every few years, someone who's not an environmental scientist announces that there is no environmental crisis, that the state of the Earth is improving, and that the future looks so rosy that our treatment of environmental resources requires – at most – minor adjustments" (Simberloff 2002). From this perspective, the linear model also confers standing on whoever has authority to participate in political debates.

Invocations of the linear model also help to some degree to explain why attacks on *TSE* became so personal and focused on

Bjørn Lomborg. Under the linear model battles over science are in effect battles over politics, and it is fair game in politics – particularly Abortion Politics – to establish the superiority of your own credentials and demolish those of your opponent in order to enhance the chances for political victory. Consider the following examples of characterizations of Lomborg made by scientists. Stephen Schneider contrasted his scientific authority with his views of Lomborg's credentials:

> For three decades, I have been debating alternative solutions for sustainable development with thousands of fellow scientists and policy analysts – exchanges carried out in myriad articles and formal meetings. . . . And who is Lomborg, I wondered, and why haven't I come across him at any of the meetings where the usual suspects debate costs, benefits, extinction rates, carrying capacity or cloud feedback? I couldn't recall reading any scientific or policy contributions from him either. (Schneider 2002)

Stuart Pimm commented, "Here's one guy taking on a whole spectrum of issues who has never written a paper on any of them and is in opposition to absolutely everyone in the field, Nobel Prize-winners and all" (in Woodard 2001). John Holdren is similarly dismissive:

> A critic has no responsibility to identify and explicate all of an author's mistakes. People with the competence needed to do this have better things to do. To explain to nonspecialists all of the mistakes in Lomborg's energy chapter would require replicating a substantial part of the introductory course on energy systems that I taught for 23 years at the University of California, Berkeley, and have now taught for 5 years at Harvard. As badly as Lomborg needs that course, I am not going to provide it for him here. (2002)

Of course, credentials were also invoked by Lomborg himself, Cambridge University Press and the media widely publicized the fact that Lomborg was a former member of Greenpeace, to underscore his environmentalist credentials. But in contrast to his critics, Lomborg downplays his scientific expertise, writing in *TSE*, "I am not myself an expert as regards environmental problems" (2001a: Preface, p. xx). And in the title of *TSE* the author presents himself as a "skeptical environmentalist" and not as a "skeptical scientist."

In places in *TSE*, Lomborg, unlike many of his critics, makes abundantly clear his political perspectives. He writes, for example, "This kind of supercilious attitude is a challenge to our democratic freedom and contests our basic right to decide for ourselves how we lead our lives, so long as doing so does not bring us into collision with others" (Lomborg 2001a: 329). And elsewhere, "We have become richer and richer primarily because of our fundamental organization in a market economy" (2001a: 351). Missed in most evaluations of *TSE*[13] is that the book is a statement about what we should value and how we should evaluate those values. At times, Lomborg contributed to such misinterpretations by couching his own analysis in the logic of the linear model.

An irony of the debate over *TSE* is that its fame owes more to its critics than to any fundamental insights of the book. Consider that sales of *TSE* quadrupled with the publication of the January 2002 issue of *Scientific American* which was critical of the book (Harrison 2004). Surely even if one rejects the critique of the linear model offered here, there is a lesson in this experience for the practicality of stealth issue advocacy in pursuit of political ends.

The case of the debate over *TSE* is an example of the general and growing problem of Stealth Issue Advocacy: through their actions, many scientists encourage the mapping of established interests from across the political spectrum onto science and then use science as a proxy for political battle over these interests. As Herrick and Jamieson (2000: 15) observe, "the imprimatur of science is being smuggled into deliberations that actually deal with values and politics." This is a familiar strategy for undergraduates in Public Policy 101 who make an argument and then seek out scientific references in support of their political views. Most of *TSE*'s critics are more subtle than undergraduate students because they focus their arguments on "science," even as they must recognize that certain scientific views are associated with certain political outcomes. But when scientists seek political outcomes through science, it can limit the positive contributions that science undoubtedly can and should make to policy development. Make no mistake, there is nothing wrong with overt political advocacy among scientists. Indeed, it is an honored role in democracies. It is when advocacy is couched in the purity of science that problems are created for both science and policy.

NINE

Making sense of science in policy and politics

The central message of this volume is that scientists have choices about if, how, and when they decide to become actively engaged in policy and politics. And how such choices are made has consequences – for individuals, the scientific enterprise as a whole, and the broader society of which they are a part. Recent times have seen increasing demands for scientists to be active in politics and policy. Each of the four idealized roles of scientists in policy and politics described in this book has its place in responding to such demands. However, it seems that one role in particular – the Issue Advocate – overwhelmingly threatens the others, particularly that of the Honest Broker of Policy Alternatives. Issue Advocacy often takes a stealth form in which scientists characterize their role as Pure Scientist or Science Arbiter, but are really using their scientific authority as a tool of advocacy.

Issue Advocates have a noble role in any democracy. Like any other citizen, scientists can of course always decide to sign up with their local political party or favorite advocacy group and lend their stature and expertise to their cause. Taking such political action lends the legitimacy and authority of science to a political cause, but it also has consequences for both science and policy. In particular, to

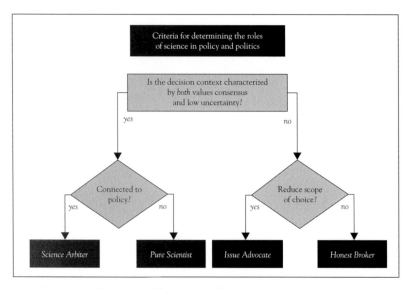

Figure 9.1 Reprisal of flow chart illustrating the logic of roles for scientists in policy and politics

the degree that science is simply mapped onto existing political perspectives we will see science overshadowed by politics, and a continued reinforcement of the twin trends of the scientization of political debate and the pathological politicization of science. When scientists align themselves with competing political perspectives, they may simply come to be viewed as an instrument of politics, and this becomes problematic when scientific information truly matters for selecting among different courses of action. In other words, it is critical to understand the differences between Abortion Politics and Tornado Politics to understand how science can play an effective role in policy and politics. Issue Advocacy, as important as it is, should always be complemented by scientists choosing to faithfully serve in each of the other roles.

Figure 9.1 reminds us of the main themes of this book in terms of the choices facing scientists and other experts when they consider how to relate their work to the needs of decision-makers. Chapter 1 suggested that such choices are grounded in broader conceptions of democracy and science. This concluding chapter builds on these concepts to summarize more general lessons for science in policy and politics based on the arguments developed in this volume.

Political context shapes the role of information in policy and politics

Science is important. It can identify when potential threats are approaching, whether the threat is a tornado approaching our location or the potential risks of climate changes a hundred years hence. But science has its limits as well. Science is of course always uncertain, particularly in highly complex, politically charged issues. But even in cases where a threat is clearly identified, science cannot tell us what to do. Deciding what to do occurs through a political process of bargaining, negotiation, and compromise. In some cases science is essential to such negotiations, and in other cases it is entirely misplaced. But whenever one invokes science (or information more generally) as a justification for selecting one course of action over others, then one is "politicizing" science. From this perspective, the politicization of science is a natural, and indeed essential, part of the political process. The beginning of understanding the difference between essential and pathological politicization lies with understanding political context.

Chapters 2 and 3 made the case that political context shapes the role of science in policy and politics. An important part of this context is the degree to which society has a sense of shared values about desirable outcomes and the means to achieve those outcomes. Where value conflicts exist, political debate thrives. Science has exceedingly little capacity to reconcile differences in values. What science can do in such situations is contribute to the development of new and innovative policy options that might allow for compromise among heretofore conflicted parties, and thus contribute also to practical action, that can occur in spite of conflict over values. This is the history of effective political action on issues such as ozone depletion and acid rain. In these cases, science did not change people's values or beliefs, but it did create new options that allowed for political compromise, given existing values and beliefs.

Chapter 7 focused on the debate over going to war in Iraq to show how political context shapes the use of science in politics. The degree of values consensus present in politics can dictate how action is to proceed in the face of irreducible uncertainty. Approaches to decision-making under uncertainty – like preemption, the precautionary principle or even "innocent until proven guilty" – work best when they reflect a shared commitment to certain values that are to be emphasized when information is uncertain. One lesson to take from the thought experiment on Tornado and Abortion Politics presented in Chapter 4 is that underlying values are important in all political contexts. It just so happens that those values can be harder to see when they are widely shared. Debates over Iraq and the precautionary principle occur in the language of information and certainty, but are really about the underlying conflict in values that results from a lack of consensus on a default course of action in the face of uncertainty. Understanding political context is essential to identifying the value of and limits to science in political conflict.

Recognize the "excess of objectivity" of science in political debate

"Science" is not a monolithic entity. Chapter 4 quoted Daniel Sarewitz who has observed that "science is sufficiently rich, diverse, and Balkanized to provide comfort and support for a range of subjective, political positions on complex issues such as climate change, nuclear waste disposal, acid rain, or endangered species" (Sarewitz 2000). Stated another way, uncertainty is often endemic and irreducible. One source of diversity in science (and hence uncertainty) stems from the perspectives of scientists themselves, as well as from the nature of the objects that they study. To take climate policy as a case in point, the scientific uncertainties are so great that it is impossible to exclude a wide range of future outcomes, ranging from relatively mild to globally catastrophic. Consequently it is easy for advocates to carefully select – to cherry pick – scientific information that supports their preferred political agenda, typically involving the Kyoto Protocol or related policies. Steve Rayner has commented that such advocacy has unnecessarily restricted debate on climate policy:

> Unfortunately, support for Kyoto has become a litmus test for determining those who take the threat of climate change seriously. But, between Kyoto's supporters and those who scoff at the dangers of leaving greenhouse gas emissions unchecked, there has been a tiny minority of commentators and analysts convinced of the urgency of the problem while remaining profoundly skeptical of the proposed solution. Their voices have largely gone unheard. Climate change policy has become a victim of the sunk costs fallacy. We are told that Kyoto is "the only game in town." However, it is plausible to argue that implementing Kyoto has distracted attention and effort from real opportunities to reduce greenhouse gas emissions and protect society against climate impacts. (Rayner 2004)

What is needed in climate policy is a greater role for Honest Brokers of Policy Alternatives. Instead the climate debate can be characterized largely in terms of stealth issue advocacy in which debates about values are thinly veiled by various competing claims about science.

Sarewitz explains that expectations that science will resolve political conflict almost always fall short because science provides an "excess of objectivity" useful in supporting a broad range of conflicting subjective positions (2000). Of course, there are cases in which science and information do matter critically in the process of deciding between alternative courses of action. This is simply because science can help us to understand the associations between different choices and their outcomes. One of the important roles of science in policy-making is thus to inform expectations about choices and their possible outcomes. Yet, science is rarely a sufficient basis for selecting among alternative courses of action because desired outcomes invariably involve differing conceptions of the sort of world we want in the future. Whether or not avoiding a particular amount of climate change is desirable, or whether or not the risks of nuclear power or GMOs exceed the benefits, are not issues that can be resolved by science alone, but must instead be handled through political processes characterized by bargaining, negotiation and compromise through the exercise of power.

Recognize the difference between seeking to reduce and seeking to expand policy choice

One way beyond the apparent limitations on the role of science in decision-making presented by conflicts over values and inherent uncertainties is to recognize that in situations of gridlock, policy-makers frequently need new options, and not more science. This lesson has been missed from the successful response to stratospheric ozone depletion. After scientists discovered in the early 1970s that human-produced chlorofluorocarbons (CFCs) could harm the ozone layer, it was not scientific information that led to political consensus. The introduction in the mid-1970s of creative policy options that distinguished essential from non-essential uses of CFCs both depoliticized the issue and stimulated the search for chemical substitutes, even as ozone science remained uncertain. In this case, scientific consensus about policy options followed a political consensus that action was needed. This lesson seems to have been lost in the current debate over climate change in which Issue Advocates battle over certainty in a misplaced effort to force a political consensus.

Expanding the options available to policy-makers is contrary to the approach most scientists have taken in the policy process when they associate themselves with a particular political agenda. Political advocacy is of course all about reducing the scope of choices, often to a single preferred vision (or candidate or policy). And the many scientists who eschew advocacy typically seek only to provide scientific information absent explicit policy context, as Pure Scientists or Science Arbiters, and stay far removed from any explicit discussion of policy options. For instance, the Intergovernmental Panel on Climate Change, which was formed to provide guidance to policymakers on climate change, by design does not discuss policy options, yet the IPCC report and its representatives often serve as Stealth Issue Advocates because some policy options are discussed and others ignored.[1]

For the protection of science and the constructive role that it can play in policy, we desperately need organizations and individuals who are willing to expand the range of options available to policy-makers by serving as Honest Brokers of Policy Alternatives. And usually there are many options consistent with sometimes internally conflicting and uncertain scientific understandings. This was once the approach of the US government's Office of Technology Assessment, but a Republican Congress, in its questionable wisdom, terminated the agency in 1995. A wide range of experiences around the world, such as that with Enquete Commissions in Europe, ought to be evaluated to assess their ability to integrate science and policy in highly political contexts (see, e.g., Juma and Yee-Cheong 2005). More organizations and individuals working from this perspective would provide a clear alternative to those from across the political spectrum who seek to politicize science in support of their own special interests.

For the consumer of scientific knowledge in the context of policy debate the following two sets of questions may be useful to ask of suppliers of policy analyses that are based on science. Asking these questions of scientists and other experts may help to encourage them to play the role of an Honest Broker of Policy Alternatives.

• If your policy recommendation is indeed based on scientific results, what scientific information would be necessary to change your policy position? (If the answer is "no information" then why depend on science at all?)

- A range of policies is consistent with particular scientific results. What is the full range of options that you see as consistent with the state of science in order to achieve particular desired ends? Within such a range, what factors other than science do you use to settle on one policy, or group of policy options, over others?

The perspective here should not be read to suggest that Issue Advocates cannot provide valuable guidance on policy. Political advocacy is in fact essential to a healthy democracy. But so too is the Honest Broker of Policy Alternatives. But the latter seems to have been overshadowed by the former. The scientific community has a responsibility for assessing the significance of science for policy, beyond merely mapping science onto its own interests. No argument is made here that such assessments offer a panacea for the challenge of decision-making in complex environmental or other scientific areas. The hope instead is that through such a process scientists themselves can work to limit the negative effects of the politicization of science and contribute to a more effective understanding of the limits of science in political debate. What makes the scientific enterprise notable is the paucity of guidance provided to policy-makers seeking to expand the available range of policy alternatives.

It is important to recognize that the Honest Broker of Policy Alternatives is very much an ideal type. In practice, having a truly comprehensive set of options would be overwhelming if not paralyzing. And any restricted set of options will necessarily reflect some value judgments as to what is included and what is not. But there is a difference between providing a single option – issue advocacy – and providing a broader set of options, particularly if the latter reflects a range of valued outcomes. Such honest brokering is far more likely to occur through the provision of advice through authoritative bodies such as international panels, professional societies, or national academies. Such bodies not only carry with them a great deal of political legitimacy, but a diversity of perspective is usually necessary to characterize a broad set of options.

The linear model of science policy has profound consequences

The linear model of science discussed in Chapters 6 and 8 is reflected in the very language that we use to discuss science and its role in society. Try to have a conversation about science in society and then observe how quickly terms arise such as "basic" and "applied." We are conditioned to think in terms of a linear relationship that gives scientists authority for making decisions about science, but creates a disconnect between science and applications or decisions. As the case study of *The Skeptical Environmentalist* suggests, when scientists seek to influence political outcomes through this model, it serves more to bring politics into science than to bring science into policy. The linear model is appealing because it provides the impression that science is somehow above or disconnected from the messiness of politics. But if people begin to see politics reflected in deliberations supposedly about science, it can work to harm the authority and legitimacy of science (Bocking 2004).

Even though scholars who study science in society have successfully critiqued as normative and descriptive theory the linear model and its implication that science and politics can be cleanly separated, it persists throughout the scientific enterprise because it reflects a perverse incentive structure that shapes science in politics. There is, to use an old political science term, an "iron triangle" of mutually reinforcing interests.

In one corner of the triangle we find the politicians who would rather not make a difficult decision, which by definition is one that will upset some part of their constituency. Consequently, the politician is more than happy to pass the onus of resolving a highly political dispute to the scientist or information broker. For example, when the administration of George W. Bush made the case for war in Iraq it based its argument on claims of danger in the form of weapons of mass destruction. Similarly, the political debate over the implications of *The Skeptical Environmentalist* took the form of debate over science. Similar examples abound. Policy-makers typically transfer responsibility to scientists (or others who collect information, such as intelligence agencies) via a large government program for research designed to provide "answers." For if the scientist can promise "answers," then the politician can avoid making the difficult decision, or at least put it off until someone else holds the policy-maker's position.

In another corner of the triangle we find the scientific community, which is to be the recipient of the tremendous resources offered by policy-makers to perform research. Not only does this research meet the desire of the research community to expand knowledge, but also, according to the politician, it has profound importance for resolving important policy issues. Two birds with one stone! The scientist thus readily accepts the generous resources for research and along with them a mandate to provide "answers."[2] The linear model helps this situation to develop. Under the linear model the scientists can claim a narrow focus only on science, because scientific results will eventually flow "downstream" to applied research and ultimately societal benefit. But under this model neither scientists nor politicians have responsibility for assessing the significance of science for policy. Hence it is left to political advocates to link science to policy, typically through political advocacy. In this way each new scientific finding is associated with a preexisting political agenda, and science is enlisted as a tool of political promotion rather than policy insight.

And thus, completing the triangle, in the third corner we find the advocate of a special interest. The advocate looks to science to provide a compelling justification for why his or her preferred policy position ought to be adopted rather than an opponent's position. As argued above, science provides a vast pool of knowledge from which information and data can be carefully cherry-picked to support a pre-determined view. The advocate's opponent thinks along the exact same lines, and also looks to invoke science in support of his or her preferred policy position. Why science? The linear model of science brings with it an air of impartiality and of being "above the fray." Ironically, the use of science in such advocacy works to undercut any claims of impartiality. Like the politician, the advocates each look to science to resolve debate; so long as the resolution is in line with the answers they already have in hand.

And so, this mutually reinforcing iron triangle of shared interests serves to replace explicit political debate about policy issues with implicit political debate shrouded in the language and practice of science. These dynamics reinforce the linear model, and in turn the linear model reinforces these dynamics, even as scholars who have studied science in society have found it to be an inaccurate description and also potentially harmful to both science and decision-making.

Institutions matter

The linear model exists both as a guiding "myth" governing the scientific enterprise, and also because institutions of science reinforce the myth (Sarewitz 1996). Government agencies, national academies, and science advisory boards all reinforce the linear model of science when they claim to focus on science absent its policy context. But over recent decades, calls for science to be more relevant to policy-making have led to institutional innovations that deviate from the linear model. Such innovations provide a useful body of experience that may help shape new approaches to science in policy and politics.

For example, in the late 1990s, the US National Science Foundation developed a second criterion (in addition to scientific excellence) for evaluating proposals based on whether the proposed research benefits society, as did various UK and international funding bodies (who ask how research can provide economic benefits). Although many scientists support this idea, many do not know how to assess the significance of their work in this way, not surprisingly, given that such assessments require a particular kind of expertise. The US National Academy of Sciences has occasionally provided such policy guidance on a range of issues, recently including arsenic in water, reproductive cloning, and streamflow for salmon and farmers, but not for many years now on policy issues related to climate change, where it has chosen to focus narrowly on science. And the US Academy certainly has a penchant for recommending "more research" as the best policy response in almost every context.

Yet authoritative and non-partisan bodies such as national science academies and societies can and should assume some responsibility for placing the significance of science into policy context. The United States used to have an institutional capacity for the provision of advice on the significance of science in its Congressional Office of Technology Assessment, which was terminated in 1995. Some, aware of the void left in OTA's absence, are currently seeking its resuscitation, but with unknown chances of success (Chubin 2000). OTA for the most part avoided partisanship in its reports by associating scientific and technological results with a wide range of possible policy outcomes, leaving to decision-makers the task of selecting particular courses of action. Given that OTA's termination was largely symbolic, having to do with Republican Congressman Newt Gingrich's promise to reduce the size of government in his "Contract With America," and the dire need in the United States for science and technology to inform policy, one might think that reviving OTA would receive serious consideration. But rather than wait for policymakers to suddenly discover the value of an OTA, the science community itself should recognize its own interests and assume some responsibility for improving the provision of policy analyses to decision-makers.

But for many the linear model remains comfortable. For instance, consider the example of appointments to science advisory committees in the United States. The US National Research Council (NRC, a body of its National Academy of Sciences) recommended in a fall 2004 report that presidential nominees to science and technology advisory panels not be asked about their political and policy perspectives; it reinforced the outmoded perspective that science and politics can be cleanly separated (National Research Council 2004). By seeking to institutionalize a clean separation of science and politics along the lines of the linear model, the NRC in effect forced the actual process of creating advisory panels into smoky backrooms and, ironically enough, all but guaranteed the continued politicization of science.

The NRC describes the political and policy perspectives of prospective panelists as "immaterial information" because such perspectives "do not necessarily predict their position on particular policies" (National Research Council 2004: 5–6). But, in reality, whether or not you ask a prospective panelist about their political or policy perspectives, for three reasons considerations of politics are simply unavoidable in the empanelment process.

First, scientists are both human beings and citizens, and as such have values and views. Frequently, scientists express these views in a public forum. Consequently, whether they are asked or not, many scientists' views on politics and policy are well known. For instance, it would be easy to convene a hypothetical advisory panel of Nobel Prize winners who happen to have signed a public letter of endorsement of John Kerry in the 2004 US presidential election without formally asking them about their political views.

Second, in just about every area except science, advisory panels, loosely described, are routinely composed with political and policy perspectives at the fore. Examples in the United States include the Supreme Court, congressional hearing witness lists, and the 9/11 Commission, to name just a few. In no other area is it even plausibly considered that politics can or should be ignored. And contrary to the assertion of the NRC, an individual's views on policy and politics do in fact shape how they think about particular issues.

Third, to evaluate whether or not a policy focused on keeping political considerations out of the scientific advisory process is actually working would require information that shows that the composition of particular panels is not biased with respect to panelists' political and policy views, which would require knowing what those views are in the first place. It is a Catch-22. Finally, it is naive to think that science advisory panels deal purely with science. Such panels are convened to provide guidance either on policy, or on scientific information that is directly relevant to policy. To suggest that policy perspectives should not be considered when creating panels to provide guidance to policy makes absolutely no sense. Rather than eliminating considerations of politics in the composition of science advisory panels, a policy of "don't ask, don't tell" would just make it more difficult to see the role played by politics, which will be ever present.

So then, what if we do allow political considerations to play a formal role in the empaneling of federal science advisory committees? Unfortunately, the situation does not get much better. In principle, government science advisory panels could be convened in much the same way that Congressional hearing witness lists are put together. That is, the majority governing party could invite some portion and the minority party could invite a portion. This could be done with parity in mind, or by giving the majority party a slight advantage. After all, the president routinely appoints people to head agencies that oversee science, based at least in part on their political perspectives. So long as the scientist in question is a world-class scientist, what would be wrong with considering their political views? All else being equal, should President George W. Bush be able to appoint a Republican scientist for a seat on a panel over a Democratic scientist?

There would be no real obstacle to implementing such a plan, as the empanelment of federal advisory committees already takes into account extra-scientific factors such as race, gender, or geographic origins of the panelists. Extra-scientific factors are considered because in almost every area of research there are far more world-class scientists than there are seats on a panel. Consequently, scientific merit alone results in a list of candidates far larger than can be seated. The government has decided that extra-scientific factors are worth considering. Political orientation could in principle be one such explicit factor. But this option also is problematic. Even in the absence of procedural obstacles, open consideration of political and policy perspectives as a criterion of empanelment would have the effect of further politicizing scientific advisory committees, because it would encourage the appointment of people with strong ideological perspectives.

But the themes developed in this book suggest that more important than the composition of the panel is the charge that it is given and the processes it employs to provide useful information to decision-makers. Debate over advisory panels' composition reinforces the old myth that we can separate science from politics, and then ensure that the science is somehow untainted by the "impurities" of the rest of society. Yet, paradoxically, we want science to be relevant to policy. A better approach would be to create institutional processes that facilitate the connections of science with policy-making, rather than trying to somehow keep them separate. Perhaps somewhat ironically, the best way to diminish the role of politics in scientific institutions is not to pretend that science and politics can be kept separate, but for such committees to openly and systematically serve as Science Arbiters when values are shared and uncertainties are low, or alternatively, as Honest Brokers of Policy Alternatives when values are in conflict and uncertainty is high.

Distinguish scientific results from their policy significance

In thinking about how things might be different, it is absolutely critical to differentiate *scientific results* from their *policy significance*. To illustrate the distinction, consider the central conclusion of the Intergovernmental Panel on Climate Change (IPCC): that global average temperature in 2100 will increase anywhere from 1.4 to 5.8 C. This is a scientific result and communication of what it means (i.e., the origins of the estimates, how "global average" is defined, the confidence level of the projection, etc.) to the non-expert may take some effort. But communication of what this result means is not the same as assessment of what it signifies for alternative courses of action. The latter is the essence of policy advice. The IPCC presents statements of trend, condition, and projection. Assessment of significance for action depends upon how trends, conditions, and projections are related to policy alternatives and their implications for valued outcomes, such as human health and environmental sustainability, as well as economic prosperity, etc. The current state of the scientific enterprise is such that the independent scientific community (i.e., those scientists without close relationships to political advocacy groups, industry, and government) typically eschews explicit discussion of the significance of science. The IPCC, for example, seeks to be "policy relevant, but policy neutral" (IPCC 2003: 2). In practice, this means that the IPCC does not consider policy alternatives and instead has institutionalized the linear model. A great irony of the IPCC process is that its institutional organization, selection of participants, and even scientific foci necessarily reflect a non-neutral policy orientation, and hence it is in fact very political (Pielke 2005).

Under the linear model, political advocates are delegated the task of interpreting the significance of science for decision-makers, and the voices of those seeking to provide guidance on policy advice are difficult for decision-makers to distinguish from those seeking to gain political advantage. So if one wishes to answer the question, "so what does this particular bit of science mean for action?" in almost any scientific context, with very few exceptions decision-makers look to political advocates for insight on the significance of science for action, in effect creating a world where almost all science is filtered through existing special interests. A better alternative is for Honest Brokers of Policy Alternatives to take some responsibility for addressing the significance for policy of scientific results. As Chapter 6 argued, such honest brokers tend to be overshadowed by political debate among competing advocates.

Who might such Honest Brokers of Policy Alternatives be? They could be individuals, but more likely will result from institutional commitments to expanding or clarifying the scope of choice available to decision-makers. Institutions can bring together people with diverse perspectives to provide a spectrum of options for decision-makers. It will be much more difficult for any one individual to serve in such a role. Honest Brokers of Policy Alternatives would not simply seek to better "communicate" the results of science to the policy-maker, or to advocate a single "best" course of action, but to develop the capability to place science into policy context, i.e., to address the question: what policy alternatives are consistent and inconsistent with scientific results? If the scientific community indeed wishes to claim independence from partisan politics, then with this comes an obligation to provide independent guidance on the significance of science for a wide scope of policy alternatives.

Ultimately, any discussion about science in policy and politics is grounded in visions of democracy

Political advocates will always seek selectively to use science in support of their agendas. This is a natural and in fact necessary part of the democratic process. However, the scientific community itself need not view this process as its only mechanism for connecting research with decision-making. The debate over *The Skeptical Environmentalist* is an extreme case that provides an opportunity for the scientific community to take a critical look at its own role in the political process and ask whether it is meeting its potential to contribute useful knowledge to policy development. Imagine if all of science in policy and politics were like the debate over *The Skeptical Environmentalist*.

To return to a theme introduced in Chapter 1, there are different visions of democracy and these different visions have profound implications for how we think about the roles of scientists and other experts. In particular, there is a profound difference between democracy as pure interest group pluralism and democracy as a competitive system in which elites bring options to the public. The former suggests that scientists ought to align themselves with their preferred political advocates and lend their expertise and legitimacy to that cause. The latter would suggest that some scientists help policy-makers and the public to understand how scientific knowledge is significant for the scope of policy choice. Individual scientists should recognize that they have choices about how they engage with policy and politics and that their perspectives on these choices will likely be shaped by their preconceptions about democracy.

With such awareness a middle ground should be seen – where some scientists resist the urge to join the political fray and instead seek through independent, authoritative bodies to provide insight that expands the choices available to policy-makers and the public, perhaps in some cases showing the way past gridlock and political stalemate, and in others offering realism about the limits of science in politics. The bottom line is that scientists have choices about how they engage the broader society of which they are a part. Hiding behind science is simply not a productive option. It is possible for those within the independent scientific community to distinguish between actions that constrain choice and those that expand the scope of choice. Making effective use of science in democracy may depend upon knowing the difference and the consequences of taking one fork in the road versus the other.

Appendix: Applying the framework

To find issues where questions arise about the appropriate roles of scientists in policy and politics, it often seems that one need only open up the morning paper. Whether the issue involves national science academies, government advisors, environmental, corporate, or other interest groups, or individual scientists, many contested public issues today involve science and scientists. To stimulate discussion and application of the framework provided in this book, this appendix provides several case studies. In each case, ask yourself,

- What decisions are faced by individual scientists or science institutions?
- And what are the consequences?
- Are the issues characterized by values conflict or consensus? Certainty or uncertainty?
- What are the consequences of serving as a Pure Scientist, Science Arbiter, Issue Advocate, or Honest Broker of Policy Alternatives?

These cases are merely a point of departure for exploring the role of scientists in policy and politics in other issue areas that you will no doubt come across just about every day.

Applying the Framework I:
Honest Brokers of Policy Alternatives

Throughout this volume has emphasized the importance of Honest Brokers of Policy Alternatives as a role for scientists and other experts in policy and politics. But who are such honest brokers?

In practice they could be any expert or collection of experts, but far more likely from the standpoints of practicality and legitimacy, Honest Brokers of Policy Alternatives will be a collection of experts on a committee or other formal organization. Such a collection may be found in a national academy or research council, as a formally established government advisory body, a working committee of a professional society, or an *ad hoc* group assembled by a public interest advocacy group. Having a diversity of perspectives reflected in clarifying or even expanding the scope of available options to decision-makers is the defining characteristic of the Honest Broker of Policy Alternatives.

A number of efforts to bring scientific and technical advice to policy-makers are worth closer examination and evaluation as candidate models for serving as Honest Brokers of Policy Alternatives. Three are discussed very briefly below.

European Enquete Commissions

In Europe, but particularly in Germany, France, Italy, and Sweden, Enquete Commissions have been used as a "common institutional forum where scientific knowledge and political judgment meet" (Krohn 2005). According to Wolfgang Krohn, "cooperation between scientists and politicians is of particular importance when the knowledge of experts is contested or uncertain and when political party lines are ill-defined with respect to an issue" – or in other words, under the criteria presented in Figure X for circumstances of values conflict and high uncertainty.

Enquete Commissions are composed of both political representatives and subject matter experts who are often appointed by the

Parliament in proportion to each party's representation. The task of an Enquete Commission is to provide a report to the Parliament with the goal of informing decision-making. In Germany, Enquete Commissions have played important roles in informing decision-making about genetic technologies and ozone depleting chemicals. Though they are not without their critics, the Enquete Commissions offer a valuable body of experience for thinking about future possibilities for honest brokering of policy alternatives.

United Kingdom Foresight

In the UK, the government's Foresight process is consistent with the notion of honest brokering of policy alternatives. Its aims are described as follows:

> A Foresight project does not predict the future, but on the basis of a thorough understanding and analysis of the subject in its broadest perspective and an awareness of different ways the future may develop identifies a range of possible outcomes. The purpose of this is to assist decision-makers now on how their decisions might affect the future, and what decisions they need to consider in the light of the possible impact the identified outcome may have on society in the future.

The Foresight project was initiated in 1994 and since then has produced more than 100 papers or reports on subjects such as infectious diseases, floods, and cyber crime. Foresight panels are sponsored by a member of Parliament, and while staffed by government officials, draw heavily on outside experts. Reports are provided to the government's chief scientific advisor. Foresight projects are uneven in their treatment of policy options, but several are notable for their discussion of a range of options, and represent a blend of technology assessment and policy analysis. The Foresight experiences provide a fertile ground for evaluating honest brokering, as well as science arbitration and the institutional and political context that facilitates each.

United States Office of Technology Assessment

The US Office of Technology Assessment (OTA) was a support agency for Congress that was terminated in 1995. OTA typically produced about fifty reports per year, each of which required about one to two years to complete. The OTA was overseen by a bipartisan board composed of members of Congress and its reports were produced by its in-house staff. The OTA often avoided a partisan flavor to its reports by presenting a range of alternatives, but this may have also contributed to perceptions that its reports were not directly useful. Some also complained that its reports were not timely enough to inform decisions. Some argued that the OTA was in fact overtly partisan, and the fact that its last director joined the Administration of Bill Clinton did little to assuage such concerns. For the most part, OTA was widely respected as a source of useful policy advice on policy issues with scientific and technological elements. Since its demise there have been calls for its recreation. While recreating OTA is perhaps unlikely, the OTA experience may offer some guidance to how the US government might more reliably encourage the honest brokering of policy alternatives on important policy issues with science and technology dimensions.

Applying the Framework II: President's Council on Bioethics

In March, 2005 *The Washington Post* reported, "Frustrated by Congress's failure to ban human cloning or place even modest limits on human embryo research, a group of influential conservatives have drafted a broad 'bioethics agenda' for President Bush's second term and have begun the delicate task of building a political coalition to support it."[1] This particular news story might not have been news if it were not for the fact that one of the leaders of this advocacy effort was none other than the sitting chair of the President's Commission on Bioethics, Leon Kass.

Irrespective of the merits of the Kass group's proposals, it would seem improper for the chair of a presidential advisory committee to also be engaging in lobbying on the same subject. Mr. Kaas was clearly trading on his position as chair of the President's Council to advance a narrow political agenda. This situation does raise questions of the roles and responsibilities of advisory committees and their members. Issue Advocates? Honest Brokers of Policy Alternatives? Science Arbiters? Clearly, they cannot serve in each role at the same time.

Mr. Kass explained to *The Washington Post* that there was no conflict of interest because money was not changing hands "Kass emphasized yesterday that his effort to craft a new legislative agenda on cloning, stem cells and related issues was independent of his role as chairman of Bush's bioethics council and that no federal resources have been used by the group, which he said has no name." Are financial commitments the only ones that matter in such circumstances? The situation is particularly of note because Mr. Kass' expertise lies in ethics.

Applying the Framework III: Hubble Space Telescope

Following the loss of the Space Shuttle Columbia, in 2004 the National Aeronautics and Space Administration (NASA) reduced the number of remaining flights for the remaining three shuttles, following the guidance of the Columbia Accident Investigation Board or CAIB). The reduction called into question the value of using one of the remaining flights to service the Hubble Space Telescope, rather than use it for some other purpose such as to complete the International Space Station.

To help select among these alternatives Senator Barbara Mikulski (D-MD) asked the NASA administrator to seek out an independent opinion. The NASA administrator returned to the CAIB which was split on whether or not to use the shuttle to service Hubble. The chairman of the CAIB responded to NASA that "whether to fly another mission to the Hubble is one of the public policy debates this nation should have," and he called for a "deep and rich study of the entire gain/risk equation (to) answer the question of whether an extension of the life of (HST) is worth the risks involved."[2] NASA responded by asking the National Research Council (NRC) to study the question.

The NRC took on the task which it characterized as "an independent assessment of options for extending the life of the Hubble Space Telescope." The Committee's formal statement of task said that it was "not expected to make either organizational or budgetary recommendations."[3] In other words, the Committee's charge set it up very much along the lines of an Honest Broker of Policy Alternatives.

What happened in practice was somewhat different. The letter report recommended that "The committee urges that NASA commit to a servicing mission to the Hubble Space Telescope" and that "NASA should take no actions that would preclude a space shuttle servicing mission to the Hubble Space Telescope." But unlike the Honest Broker of Policy Alternatives, these recommendations represent a narrowing of the scope of choice, more consistent with the Issue Advocate.

That the influential committee advocated saving Hubble and using the Shuttle to do so is perhaps not surprising when one considers its composition. The very distinguished panel included many people with a direct interest in Hubble:[4]

- A former director of the Space Telescope Science Institute which manages Hubble.
- A space scientist who has criticized how human spaceflight programs took money from programs such as Hubble
- A scientist who serves on a council that helps to manage Hubble
- An astronaut who helped deploy Hubble from the space shuttle
- Several former NASA employees

- A scientist whose work depends upon Hubble
- A scientist who advocates for space telescope missions.

Was the membership commensurate with the task facing the Committee? How else might have it been empanelled?

Applying the Framework IV:
Hurricanes and political self-segregation

During 2005 and 2006 intense debate raged among scientists about the possible role of human-caused climate change in hurricane activity. Scientists participating in this debate often turned to advocacy groups to amplify their perspectives. Such stealth issue advocacy by scientists arguably contributed to the pathological politicization of climate science.

For example, in the spring of 2006, a group of scientists were promoted by a group called TCS – Tech Central Station – which values "the power of free markets, open societies and individual human ingenuity to raise living standards and improve lives."[5] Each of the scientists cited in the TCS press release believes that global warming plays little discernible role in hurricane activity.

Consider another example from the other side of the debate. Late in the summer of 2006 another group of scientists collaborated with an environmental group to promote research suggesting that sea surface temperatures had increased due to global warming.[6] Each of these scientists believes that global warming is the primary reason behind increased hurricane activity.

Interest groups have a great deal of power in such situations, because they can selectively assemble experts on any given topic to basically support any ideological position. This is a function of what Dan Sarewitz calls an "excess of objectivity." That interest groups will cherrypick among experts comes as no surprise, but what, if any, responsibility do scientists have in such advocacy and what are the implications for the scientific enterprise?

From the perspective of the individual scientist deciding to align with an interest group, it should be recognized that such a decision is political. There is of course nothing wrong with politics, it is how we get the business of society done, and organized interest groups are fundamental to modern democracy. Nonetheless, an observer of this dynamic might be forgiven for thinking when on a particular issue they see many or even most scientists self-select and organize themselves according to political predispositions that different perspectives on scientific issues are simply a function of political ideologies. We often see how contentious political debates involving science become when filtering science through interest groups is the dominant mechanism for connecting science to policy.

It is this condition of dueling special interest scientists that leads to a second perspective, and that is an institutional approach to providing science advice in a way that is not filtered through a particular special interest agenda. It is this very condition that gives legitimacy to government science advisory panels, National Academy committees, and professional societies. When scientists organize to serve as Honest Brokers of Policy Alternatives it can serve to militate against the pathological politicization of science.

Applying the Framework V: Perchlorate and science arbitration

In January 2005 the National Research Council released a report on the "Health Implications of Perchlorate Ingestion." The study was significant because, as The New York Times reported, "Depending on how federal and state regulators interpret the academy's recommendation, the Defense Department, its contractors and other federal agencies responsible for contamination from perchlorate, a component of solid rocket fuel, could avoid cleanup costs of hundreds of millions of dollars."[7] The political stakes are very high.

An investigation of the report by the National Resources Defense Council (NRDC) illustrates the challenges in setting up a process that enables effective science arbitration. NRDC found that "the NAS panel's recommendation was likely shaped by a covert campaign by the White House, Pentagon and defense contractors to twist the science and strong-arm the academy."[8] In other words, the NRC report reflects the results of political pressure and maneuvering by Bush Administration officials. Specifically, the NRDC found:

(1) "senior White House officials reviewed and apparently edited a highly technical document charging NAS with evaluating detailed scientific questions."

This is significant because the charge given to a committee dictates its scope and how questions are framed. Often the framing of questions bounds the range of policy recommendations that result. What is missing in the NRC is an open and transparent process for developing a charge to its committees. If the executive branch officials, both in agencies and the White House, who are paying for the study, are responsible for developing with NRC staff the committee's charge, then we should fully expect that the charge will be slanted toward the political views of those funding the study. One option would be for the NRC to require politically charged issues to be funded by a diversity of parties. For example, NRDC could have been invited to be a co-sponsor of the study and thus be allowed to participate in the development of the charge. This may not always be a simple solution, as the government has deep pockets and advocacy groups often do not. But in this case this would have allowed for political compromises to be reached between NRDC and the Bush Administration well before bringing in the experts to answer technical questions.

(2) "the White House, Pentagon and DOD contractors sought to manipulate the panel's membership to place 'friendly' scientists on it."

Just like in the development of the charge, the composition of the panel can easily be "stacked" in one direction or another. Such stacking would be less likely if those responsible for funding the study reflected a diverse set of interests. It is hopeless to think that there are unbiased or objective scientists who are untainted by politics out there who could have been placed on this panel. But dealing with the issue of the panel's composition before submitting the technical questions would have gone a long way toward increasing the legitimacy of the report's conclusions. By relying only on the Bush Administration for funding for this study, the NRC opened the door to an undue influence from one political perspective over others.

All of this suggests that the advisory panels need to take a long hard look at their efforts to connect scientific advice with the needs of policy-makers. The NRC faces an inherent conflict because its studies are paid for by the folks to whom it is providing advice. It can to some degree deal with this by requiring a diversity of funding sources for particular studies and allowing these diverse participants to collectively reach agreement on a committee's charge and composition. The alternative is that we see the political battles fought either inside the NRC committee or in the public after it is released, which in both cases will diminish the positive role of science arbiters in contributing to policy.

Notes

1. FOUR IDEALIZED ROLES OF SCIENCE IN POLICY AND POLITICS

1. There are obviously complexities here. For example, when goals are not shared among different participants in a political process, one acts more like an Honest Broker of Policy Alternatives when presenting available options for both ends and means. When goals are shared, the task of honest brokering can focus more exclusively on means. One can also be an Issue Advocate for ends (e.g., ending poverty) and an Honest Broker of Policy Alternatives on means (e.g., alternative actions available to achieve the goal of ending poverty).

2. This phrase will be discussed in some greater detail in Chapter 6. For the phrase itself I am indebted to Lackey (2004).

3. Of course, pure science (as well as science focused on practical questions) can and frequently does point to the existence of a problem that compels action, but introducing reasons that might suggest the need for possible action is quite different from providing guidance on what actions to actually take in specific circumstances.

4. I borrow this phrase from Armstrong (2002).

5. Some scientists will respond that they do not have expertise in decision-making or policy and thus cannot make such associations. The reply, of course, is that scientists need to either broaden their expertise or seek out collaborators who have the requisite knowledge and experience.

2. THE BIG PICTURE, SCIENCE, AND DEMOCRACY

1. See, for example, Jasanoff *et al.* (1995). No such similar overview exists for STP.

2. The quotes here are as reported by Freese (2006).

3. This "is–ought problem" is described in the context of the climate debate in *The science and politics of climate change: a guide to the debate* (Dessler and Parson 2005).

4. Many scientists' views of science in decision-making are consistent with the notion of Science Arbiter as presented here (cf. Dessler and Parson 2005). More generally, most calls for scientific assessments or scientific advice invoke the scientist as arbiter of positive questions. As will be seen, this is a difficult role to play and in practice often takes the form of explicit or implicit issue advocacy.

3. SCIENCE AND DECISION-MAKING

1. The word "policy" has many definitions in the literature, sometimes being used to refer exclusively to governmental decisions. The definition used here is much broader. The purpose of defining policy here is simply for the reader to know what I mean when I use the term.

2. Those interested in the most up-to-date answer to this question from the US government should consult the website of the National Institutes of Health: www.nci.nih.gov/cancertopics/pdq/screening/breast/patient.

3. Another political scientist of the twentieth century, David Easton (1965: 96), provided a compatible definition: politics involves "those patterns of interaction through which values are allocated for a society and these allocations are accepted as authoritative by most persons in the society most of the time."

4. VALUES

1. Consider that in some languages there is one word for both policy and politics. This can be overcome by recognizing that, at least as used in this book, the word "policy" is simply a synonym for the word "decision."

2. Readers familiar with the STS literature will recognize the influence on this chapter of the concepts of "normal" and "post-normal" science discussed by Funtowicz and Ravetz (e.g., 1992).

3. By contrast, when a very rare tornado appeared over Boulder, Colorado in 1996 while I worked at the National Center for Atmospheric Research, most of my colleagues headed to the roof rather than the basement!

4. Also for the purposes of this thought experiment, to keep things simple, please consider those individuals whose abortion views are a function of the viability of a fetus as willing to accept abortion under certain conditions.

5. This perspective is consistent with the work of George Lakoff (2004).

6. Consider what scientific information would make you change your own views on abortion, whatever those views happen to be.

7. In May 2005, President Bush restated his opposition to federal funding of embryonic stem-cell research.

5. UNCERTAINTY

1. Compare the view of political scientist Anthony Downs, "uncertainty is so basic to human life that it influences the structure of almost every social institution" (1957: 88).
2. A "measurand" is a physical parameter being quantified by measurement.
3. Compare Keynes (1937: 214), "[Under uncertainty] there is no scientific basis on which to form any calculable probability whatever. We simply do not know. Nevertheless, the necessity for action and for decision compels us as practical men to do our best to overlook this awkward fact and to behave exactly as we should if we had behind us a good Benthamite calculation of a series of prospective advantages and disadvantages, each multiplied by its appropriate probability waiting to be summed."
4. The story of Long Term Capital Management is by no means unique in the annals of finance, see, e.g., Chancellor (1999).
5. This case is described in Eskeland and Feyzioglu (1995).
6. A related consideration is that attempts to eliminate uncertainty by changing thresholds for decision (e.g., changing the wind-speed criteria for evacuation) invariably result in trade-offs between false alarms and misses (i.e., Type I and Type II errors), with associated societal costs. See Stewart (2000).
7. For those unfamiliar with the game, each player is dealt five cards, with the object to obtain cards ranking higher than those of the other players. After the initial deal of five cards per player, each player has the option to exchange up to three cards. The poker statistics reported in this section are taken from Scarne (1986).
8. There are other sources of irreducible uncertainty; some of these are discussed below.
9. In a very similar fashion some studies of global climate change use such a method to assess whether the storms, temperature, precipitation, etc. of one period differ significantly from those of another period (compare Wunsch 1999).
10. Compare Oreskes et al. (1994).

6. HOW SCIENCE POLICY SHAPES SCIENCE IN POLICY AND POLITICS

1. To be sure, critiques of the linear model have a history going back almost as far as Vannevar Bush's original report (1945) which successfully placed the linear model at the center of thinking about science policy.

2. Scholars of innovation have long recognized that the linear model provides an inadequate description of how things actually work in practice. See, e.g., Rosenberg (1982).
3. Polanyi and J. D. Bernal engaged in a debate over science policy that continues to shape discussions of science policy today. See Brown (2005).
4. We also see this discussion reflected in literature on science policy. For instance, see Cash et al. (2003); Guston (2001); Jasanoff (1990); Nowotny et al. (2001).
5. There have been some notable challenges to post-war science policy, but arguably nothing of the sort seen since the end of the Cold War.

7. PREEMPTION AND THE DECISION TO GO TO WAR IN IRAQ

1. There is a large literature on the legitimizing role of science in information-based controversies. See, e.g., Oreskes (2004).
2. Armstrong gained some notoriety in 2005 during the confirmation hearings of John Bolton to serve as US ambassador to the United Nations. Armstrong was identified as an analyst that Bolton sought to pressure to modify his intelligence analysis to better suit Bolton's political agenda.
3. And compare Armstrong's views with the quote from Lord May on p. v of this book.
4. The so-called "Downing Street Memo" released to the public in May 2005, supports this interpretation (Danner 2005). The memo states, "Military action was now seen as inevitable. Bush wanted to remove Saddam, through military action, justified by the conjunction of terrorism and WMD. But the intelligence and facts were being fixed around the policy" (2005).
5. See also Hammond (1962).
6. The Clinton-era policy of "enlargement" as described here is based on the remarks of Anthony Lake (1993). An excellent resource for period documents on US foreign policy is the home page of Professor Vincent Ferraro (2006) at Mount Holyoke College.
7. Additional documentation on the national security policies of the Bush administration can be found at http://www.mtholyoke.edu/acad/intrel/bush/doctrine.htm.
8. This conclusion should be robust to one's feelings about the merit of the war itself.

8. WHEN SCIENTISTS POLITICIZE SCIENCE

1. See, e.g., Jasanoff and Wynne (1998), and the extensive list of references therein.

2. For example, in the United States the reports of Congressman Henry Waxman and the Union of Concerned Scientists focus on the politicization of science by elected and appointed officials, and not the politicization of science by scientists (Union of Concerned Scientists 2003; US House of Representatives Committee on Government Reform 2003).

3. A similar thesis has been presented by Ronald Bailey (1993) and Greg Easterbrook (1995).

4. To be sure, the challenge of special interests for democracy has long been a concern associated with democratic governance. See, e.g., in a US context James Madison (1787), writing in *Federalist 10*. I do not take on this general challenge focusing instead on the politicization of science by scientists as a particular instance of the politics of interests. See, e.g., Petracca (1992).

5. Compare, Oreskes (2004); Sarewitz (2004).

6. For several examples see the white papers prepared for the Union of Concerned Scientists, an advocacy group, by Peter Gleick, of the Pacific Institute for Studies in Development, Environment, and Security, and Jerry Mahlman, former director of the US government's Geophysical Fluid Dynamics Laboratory (Union of Concerned Scientists 2003).

7. Transcript of The Science Show on Australian Radio National, Robyn Williams, Bjørn Lomborg, and Peter Raven (Radio National 2002).

8. For an insider's perspective of TSE see the article by its editor, Harrison (2004).

9. On this see the charges leveled by WRI and Lomborg's response (Lomborg 2001b).

10. Compare also the World Bank/WWF Forest Alliance (World Bank Group 2003).

11. Other factors besides politics motivated critics of TSE. For example, John Holdren (2002) wrote of the "anger and, yes, contempt" expressed by some scientists that Lomborg violated professional norms of conduct. Personality and ego considerations, while certainly real, do not vitiate the argument presented here.

12. A recent study of the role of the media in shaping opinions provides support for the claim that both sides of the debate over TSE are simply wrong in their expectation that the outcome of their public debate will compel certain policies. See, Besley and Shanahan (2004).

13. But not all; see Oreskes (2004).

9. MAKING SENSE OF SCIENCE IN POLICY AND POLITICS

1. For instance, the IPCC strongly favors mitigation responses to climate change over adaptive responses. See Pielke (2005).

2. Substantial research funding creates its own political constituency (see Pielke and Sarewitz 2003).

APPENDIX: APPLYING THE FRAMEWORK

1. www.washingtonpost.com/wp-dyn/articles/A15569-2005Mar7.html
2. http://darwin.nap.edu/openbook.php?record_id=11051&page=8
3. http://darwin.nap.edu/books/NI000551/html/9.html
4. http://sciencepolicy.colorado.edu/prometheus/archives/space_policy/
   000134nrc_report_on_hubble.html
5. www.tcsdaily.com/about.aspx
6. www.chron.com/disp/story.mpl/front/4179513.html
7. www.nytimes.com/2005/01/11/politics/11report.html
8. www.nrdc.org/media/pressreleases/050110.asp

References

AAAS 1960. "Science and human welfare: The AAAS Committee on science in the promotion of human welfare states the issues and calls for action," *Science* 32: 68–73.

Andersen, Stephen O. and Madhava Sarma, K. 2002. *Protecting the ozone layer: the United Nations history*. London: Earthscan Publications.

Armstrong, Fulton T. 2002. "Ways to make analysis relevant but not prescriptive," *Studies in Intelligence* 46 (3), www.cia.gov/csi/studies/vol46no3/article05.html.

Armstrong, John A. 1994. "Is basic research a luxury our society can no longer afford?," *The Bridge* (Summer): 9–16.

Aron, William, Burke, W., and Freeman, M. 2002. "Scientists versus whaling: science, advocacy and errors of judgment," *Bioscience* 52: 1137–1140.

Bailey, Ronald 1993. *Eco-scam: the false prophets of ecological apocalypse*. New York: St. Martin's Press.

Bernstein, Peter L. 1996. *Against the gods: the remarkable story of risk*. New York: John Wiley and Sons.

Besley, John C. and Shanahan, James 2004. "Skepticism about media effects concerning the environment: examining Lomborg's hypotheses," *Society and Natural Resources* 17 (10): 861–880.

Betsill, Michele M. 2001. "Mitigating climate change in US cities: opportunities and obstacles," *Local Environment* 6 (4): 393–406, www.colostate.edu/Depts/PoliSci/fac/mb/Local%2oEnvironment.pdf.

Bimber, Bruce 1996. *The politics of expertise in Congress: the rise and fall of the Office of Technology Assessment*. Albany, NY: State University of New York Press.

Blair, Tony 2003. "Speech before joint session of the United States Congress," July 17, edition.cnn.com/2003/US/07/07/blair.transcript/.

Bocking, Stephen 2004. *Nature's experts: science, politics, and the environment*. New Brunswick: Rutgers University Press.

Bode, Hendrik W. 1964. "Reflections on the relation between science and technology," in US House of Representatives, Committee on Science and Technology, *Basic research and national goals: a report to the Committee on Science and Astronautics*, pp. 41–76.

Bozeman, Barry 1977. "A governed science and a self-governing science: the conflicting values of autonomy and accountability," in Joseph Haberer (ed.), *Science and technology policy: perspectives and developments*. Lexington, MA: Lexington Books, pp. 55–66.

Branscomb, Lewis M. 1992. "Does America need a technology policy," *Harvard Business Review* 70: 24–31.

Brooks, Harvey 1964. "The scientific advisor," in Robert Gilpin and Christopher, Wright (eds.), *Scientists and national policy-making*. New York: Columbia University Press, pp. 73–96.

1995. "The evolution of US science policy," in Bruce L. R. Smith and Claude E. Barfield (eds.), *Technology, R&D, and the economy*. Washington, DC: The Brookings Institution.

Brown, Andrew 2005. *J.D. Bernal: the sage of science*. New York: Oxford University Press.

Brown, George E., Jr. 1992. "Guest comment: the objectivity crisis," *American Journal of Physics* 60 (9): 779–781.

Burden, Barry C. (ed.) 2003. *Uncertainty in American politics*. Cambridge: Cambridge University Press.

Bush, George W. 2002a. "Remarks by President Bush at 2002 graduation exercise of the United States Military Academy," West Point, New York. June 1, www.mtholyoke.edu/acad/intrel/bush/westpoint.htm.

2002b. "President's remarks at the United Nations General Assembly," September 12, www.whitehouse.gov/news/releases/2002/09/20021912-0.html.

2003. "President delivers 'State of the Union'," January 28, www.whitehouse.gov/news/releases/2003/01/20030128-19.html.

Bush, Vannevar 1945. *Science – the endless frontier*. Washington, DC: Government Printing Office (reprinted 1960).

Cash, David W., Clark, William C., Alcock, Frank, Dickson, Nancy M., Eckley, Noelle, Guston, David H., Jäger, Jill, and Mitchell, Ronald B. 2003. "Knowledge systems for sustainable development," *Proceedings of the National Academy of Sciences of the United States of America* 100 (14): 8086–8091, www.pnas.org/cgi/reprint/100/14/8086.pdf.

CBS News 2003. "Poll: Americans see long stay in Iraq," April 28, www.cbsnews.com/stories/2003/04/28/opinion/polls/main551377.shtml.

Cetacean Society International 2003. "Cetacean news," *Whales Alive!* 12 (4), csiwhalesalive.org/csi03402.html.

Chancellor, Edward 1999. *Devil take the hindmost: a history of financial speculation.* New York: Farrar, Straus, and Giroux.

Chubin, Daryl E. 2000. "Filling the policy vacuum created by OTA's demise," *Issues in Science and Technology Policy*, Winter, www.nap.edu/issues/17.2/stalk.htm.

Clarke, Tom 2003. "Whale numbers disputed," *Nature*, July 25, www.nature.com/news/2003/030721/full/030721-14.html.

Clymer, Adam 2002. "US revises sex information, and a fight goes on," *The New York Times*, December 27: A15.

CNN 2003. "Chirac: Iraq war undermined U.N.," September 23, cnn.com/2003/US/09/23/sprj.irq.annan/index.html.

Collins, Simon 2003. "Climate study just hot air say critics," *The New Zealand Herald*, August 7, www.nzherald.co.nz/storydisplay.cfm?storyID=3516830&msg=emaillink.

Custred, Glynn 2002. "The Kennewick man case," National Association of Scholars, *Science Insights* 7 (1), www.nas.org/publications/sci newslist/7 1/d kennewick artic.htm.

Daddario, Emilio 1974. "Science and policy: relationships are the key," *Daedalus* 103 (Summer): 140.

Daniels, George H. 1967. "The pure-science ideal and democratic culture," *Science* 156: 1699–1705.

Danish Committees on Scientific Dishonesty. 2003. Decision regarding complaints against Bjørn Lomborg, Danish Research Agency, January 7, www.cambridge.org/uk/economics/lomborg/files/DRA_Decision.pdf.

Danner, Mark 2005. "The secret way to war," *The New York Review of Books* 52 (10), www.nybooks.com/articles/18034.

Dessler, Andrew E. and Parson, Edward A. 2005. *The science and politics of climate change: a guide to the debate.* Cambridge: Cambridge University Press.

Dewey, John 1997. *How we think.* Mineola, NY: Dover Publications (originally published 1910).

Dionne, Eugene J. 2003. "Wrong path to war," *The Washington Post*, October 7, A25, www.washingtonpost.com/ac2/wp-dyn/A53170-2003Oct6.

Dobbs, Michael 2003. "N. Korea tests Bush's policy of preemption," *The Washington Post*, January 6: A01, www.washingtonpost.com/ac2/wp-dyn/A14613-2003Jan5.

Dower, Roger, Ditz, Daryl, Faeth, Paul, Johnson, Nels, Kozloff, Keith, and MacKenzie, James J. 1997. *Frontiers of sustainability: environmentally sound agriculture, forestry, transportation, and power production.* Washington, DC: Island Press.

Downs, Anthony 1957. *An economic theory of democracy.* New York: HarperCollins.

Dubos, René 1961. "Scientist and public: why is the scientist, once a 'natural philosopher,' now considered a barbarian by many educated laymen?," *Science* 133: 1207–1211, www.sciencemag.org/cgi/reprint/133/3460/1207.pdf.

Dupree, A. Hunter 1957. *Science in the federal government: a history of policies and activities to 1940.* Cambridge, MA: Belknap Press of Harvard University Press.

Easterbrook, Gregg 1995. *A moment on the earth: the coming age of environmental optimism.* New York: Viking Press.

Easton, David 1965. *A framework for political analysis.* Englewood Cliffs, NJ: Prentice-Hall.

The Economist 2001. "Doomsday postponed," *The Economist*, September 6, www.economist.com/printedition/displaystory.cfm?story_id=770765.

2006. "The global nuclear energy partnership: reactor dreams," *The Economist*, February 23, www.economist.com/displayStory.cfm?story_id=5558922.

EPA 2006. "Role of science at EPA," US Environmental Protection Agency, www.epa.gov/osp/science.htm.

Eskeland, Gunner S. and Feyzioglu, Tarhan 1995. "Rationing can backfire: the 'day without a car' in Mexico City," *The World Bank Economic Review* 11 (3): 383–408, www.worldbank.org/research/journals/wber/revsep97/pdf/article1.pdf.

Everything Atkins 2002. "Low carb food pyramid," Everything Atkins, www.everythingatkins.net/LCpyramid.html.

Ferraro, Vincent 2006. "Home page of Professor Vincent Ferraro," The Ruth C. Lawson Professor of International Politics, Mount Holyoke College, www.mtholyoke.edu/acad/intrel/feros-pg.htm.

Freese, Duane D. 2006. "Science in the house of pain," *TecCentralStation*, July 26, www.tcsdaily.com/article.aspx?id=072606G.

Funtowicz, Silvio O. and Ravetz, Jerome R. 1992. "Three types of risk assessment and the emergence of post-normal science," in Sheldon Krimsky and Dominic Golding (eds.), *Social theories of risk.* New York: Praeger, pp. 251–273.

Gellman, Barton and Pincus, Walter 2003. "Depiction of threat outgrew supporting evidence," *The Washington Post*, August 10: A01, www.washingtonpost.com/ac2/wp-dyn?pagename=article&contentId=A39500-2003Aug9.

Georghiou, Luke 1996. "The UK technology foresight programme," *Futures* 28: 359–377.

Gephardt, Richard 2002. "Defend the country, not the party," *The New York Times*, September 27: A31.

Gillies, Donald 2000. *Philosophical theories of probability*. New York and London: Routledge Press.

Goldstein, Andrew 2002. "Reviled for sticking it to ecological dogma, Bjørn Lomborg laughs all the way to the bank," *Time*, August 18, www.time.com/time/2002/greencentury/enlomborg.html.

Gomory, Ralph 1990. "Of ladders, cycles and economic growth," *Scientific American* (June): 140.

Goodell, Jeff 2001. "Judas among the tree-huggers," *Rolling Stone*, October 11: 47–48.

Gough, Michael (ed.) 2003. *Politicizing science: the alchemy of policymaking*. Stanford, CA: Hoover Institution Press.

Gray, Thomas 1747. "Ode on a distant prospect of Eton College," London: Printed for R. Dodsley, Online text 2005, Ian Lancashire for the Department of English, University of Toronto, http://rpo.library.utoronto.ca/poem/884.html.

Greenberg, Daniel S. 2001. *Science, money, and politics: political triumph and ethical erosion*. Chicago: University of Chicago Press.

Guston, David H. 2000. "Retiring the social contract for science," *Issues in Science and Technology*, Summer, www.nap.edu/issues/16.4/p_guston.htm.

2001. "Boundary organizations in environmental policy and science: an introduction," *Science, Technology & Human Values* 26 (4): 399–408, http://sth.sagepub.com/cgi/reprint/26/4/399.

Guston, David H. and Kensiton, Kenneth 1994. *The fragile contract: university science and the federal government*. Cambridge, MA: MIT Press.

Hammond, Kenneth R. 1996. *Human judgment and social policy: irreducible uncertainty, inevitable error, unavoidable injustice*. New York: Oxford University Press.

Hammond, Paul Y. 1962. "NSC-68: prologue to rearmament," in Schilling, Warner R., Hammond, Paul Y. and Snyder, Glenn, *Strategy, politics, and defense budgets*. New York: Columbia University Press, pp. 267–378.

Harrison, Chris 2004. "Peer review, politics, and pluralism," *Environmental Science & Policy* 7 (5): 357–368.

Hart, Gary and Rudman, Warren B. 2002. *America – still unprepared, still in danger*. New York: Council on Foreign Relations, www.cfr.org/content/publications/attachments/Homeland_TF.pdf.

HCSST 1989. "The Global Change Research Act of 1989," House Committee on Science, Space, and Technology 101: 74, July 27.

Herrick, Charles N. and Jamieson, Dale 2000. "Junk science and environmental policy: obscuring public debate with misleading discourse," *Philosophy and Public Policy Quarterly* 21 (2/3):11–16, www.publicpolicy.umd.edu/IPPP/reports/Spring-Summer%20Vol21%202001/221056.pdf.

Hoffman, F. Owen and Hammonds, Jana S. 1994. "Propagation of uncertainty in risk assessments: the need to distinguish between uncertainty due to lack of knowledge and uncertainty due to variability," *Risk Analysis* 14: 707–712.

Hoge, Warren 2003. "Blair draws heat from former aides on Iraq arms," *International Herald Tribune*, June 18.

Holdren, John P. 2002. "A response to Bjørn Lomborg's response to my critique of his energy chapter," *Scientific American*, April 15, www.sciam.com/print_version.cfm?articleID=000DC658-9373-1CDA-B4A8809EC588EEDF.

2003. "Politics and science: letters to the editor," *International Herald Tribune*, January 28, www.iht.com/articles/2003/01/28/edlet_ed3__31.php.

Huxley, Thomas Henry 1882. *Science and culture, and other essays.* New York: D. Appleton and Company.

Immelt, Jeff 2005. "Global environmental challenges lecture," George Washington School of Business, May 9, www.ge.com/files/usa/company/news/global_environmental_challenges.pdf.

IPCC 2003. "Procedures for the preparation, review, acceptance, adoption, approval and publication of IPCC reports," Fifteenth Session of the IPCC (San Jose, April 15–18, 1999) and revised, on a provisional basis, at the Twentieth Session of the IPCC (Paris, February 19–21, 2003), www.climatescience.gov/Library/ipcc/app-a.pdf.

IWMC 2003. "Flawed science fails acceptance," *Sustainable eNews*, August, www.iwmc.org/newsletter/2003/2003-08-07.htm.

Jasanoff, Sheila S. 1987. "Contested boundaries in policy-relevant science," *Social Studies of Science* 17 (2): 195–230.

1990. *The fifth branch: science advisors as policy-makers.* Cambridge, MA: Harvard University Press.

Jasanoff, Sheila S. and Wynne, Brian 1998. "Science and decisionmaking," in Steve Rayner, Elizabeth L. Malone (eds.), *Human choice and climate change, vol. 1: The societal framework.* Columbus, OH: Battelle Press, pp. 1–87.

Jasanoff, Sheila S., Markle, Gerald E., Peterson, James C., and Pinch, Trevor J. (eds.) 1995. *Handbook of science and technology studies.* Thousand Oaks, CA: Sage Publications.

Johnson, George 2002. "To err is human," *The New York Times*, July 14: 4.1.

Juma, Calestous and Yee-Cheong, Lee 2005. *Innovation: applying knowledge in development.* United Nations Development Programme. London: Earthscan, www.unmillenniumproject.org/documents/Science-complete. pdf.

Kantrowitz, Arthur 1994. "Elitism vs. checks and balances in communicating scientific information to the public," *Risk: Health, Safety and the Environment* 4: 101–111, www.piercelaw.edu/risk/vol4/spring/kantro.htm.

Kennan, George (signed as X.) 1947. "The sources of Soviet conduct," *Atlantic Monthly*, www.historyguide.org/europe/kennan.html.

Keynes, John Maynard 1937. "The general theory of employment," *Quarterly Journal of Economics* 51 (2): 209–223.

Kidd, Charles V. 1959. "Basic research – description versus definition: a definition of basic research in probability terms is useful, but statistics based theron are not," *Science* 129: 368–371.

Kitcher, Philip 2001. *Science, truth, and democracy*. New York: Oxford University Press.

Kline, Stephen J. 1985. "Innovation is not a linear process," *Research Management* 28 (4): 36–45.

Kolata, Gina 2002. "The nation: second opinion: the painful fact of medical uncertainty," *The New York Times*, February10: I5, http://query.nytimes.com/gst/fullpage.html?sec=health&res=9500E1D8153CF933A25751C0A9649C8B63.

Kolata, Gina and Moss, Michael 2002. "X-Ray vision in hindsight: science, politics and the mammogram," *The New York Times*, February11: A23, query.nytimes.com/gst/fullpage.html?sec=health&res=9B05EFDD103CF932A25751C0A9649C8B63.

Krohn, Wolfgang 2005. "Enquete commissions," in Carl Mitcham (ed.), *Encyclopedia of Science, Technology, and Ethics*. Farmington Hills, MI: Macmillan Reference USA, pp. 641–644.

Lackey, Robert T. 2004. Normative science. *Fisheries* 29 (7): 38–39.

Lake, Anthony 1993. "From containment to enlargement," September 21, Johns Hopkins University, www.mtholyoke.edu/acad/intrel/lakedoc.html.

Lakoff, George 2004. *Don't think of an elephant! Know your values and frame the debate*. White River Junction, VT: Chelsea Green Publishing.

Lasswell, Harold Dwight 1958. *Politics: who gets what, when, how*. New York: Meridian Press.

Lasswell, Harold Dwight and Kaplan, Abraham 1950. *Power and society: a framework for political inquiry*. New York: Yale University Press.

Lee, Jennifer 2003. "A call for softer, greener language," *The New York Times*, March 2: 24, www.luntzspeak.com/graphics/NewYorkTimes.NewsStory.pdf.

Lempert, Robert J. 2000. "Robust strategies for abating climate change," *Climatic Change* 45 (1): 387–401.

Lomborg, Bjørn 2001a. *The skeptical environmentalist: measuring the real state of the world*. New York: Cambridge University Press.

2001b. "Bjørn Lomborg's comments on the critique by World Resources Institute and World Wildlife Fund," December 17, www.lomborg.com/files/Response%20to%20WRI-WWF3.pdf.

Lovejoy, Thomas 2002. "Biodiversity: dismissing scientific process," *Scientific American*, January, www.sciam.com/article.cfm?articleID=000F3D47-C6D2-1CEB-93F6809EC5880000&pageNumber=9&catID=2.

Lowenstein, Roger 2000. *When genius failed: the rise and fall of Long-Term Capital Management*. New York: Random House.

Madison, James 1787. "The *Federalist* no. 10: the utility of the union as a safeguard against domestic faction and insurrection," *Daily Advertiser*, November 22, www.constitution.org/fed/federa10.htm.

Mahlman, Jerry D. 2001. "Global warming: misuse of data and ignorance of science, a review of the "Global warming" chapter of Bjørn Lomborg's the skeptical environmentalist: measuring the real state of the world," Union of Concerned Scientists, December 6, www.ucsusa.org/assets/documents/global_warming/ACFCGy9yc.pdf.

Mann, William C. 2003. "Democratic senators denounce Bush's performance as war president," *San Francisco Chronicle*, October 12, www.dailytimes.com.pk/default.asp?page=story_14-10-2003_pg4_6.

Marris, Emma 2006. "Should conservation biologists push policies?," *Nature* 442 (13), www.nature.com/nature/journal/v442/n7098/full/442013a.html.

Mestel, Rosie 2004. "We eat: therefore, they are," *Los Angeles Times*, August 10: A.1.

Michaels, David, Bingham, Eula, Boden, Les, Clapp, Richard, Goldman, Lynn R., Hoppin, Polly, Krimsky, Sheldon, Monforton, Celeste, Ozonoff, David, and Robbins, Anthony 2002. "Advice without dissent," *Science* 298: 703, www.sciencemag.org/cgi/reprint/298/5594/703.pdf.

Monastersky, Richard 2003. "Storm brews over global warming," *The Chronicle of Higher Education* 50 (2): A16, http://chronicle.com/weekly/v50/i02/02a01601.htm.

National Research Council 2004. *Science and technology in the national interest: ensuring the best presidential and federal advisory committee science and technology appointments*. Washington, DC: National Academy Press, http://books.nap.edu/html/national-interest/1-10.pdf.

National Science Board 1996. *Science and engineering indicators – 1996*. Washington, DC: US Government Printing Office, NSB 96–21, www.nsf.gov/statistics/seind96/sepdf.htm.

Nature Publishing Group 2002. "Cloning conundrums," *Nature Medicine* 8 (12): 1331, www.nature.com/nm/journal/v8/n12/full/nm1202-1331.html.

Nestle, Marion 2002. *Food politics: how the food industry influences nutrition and health*. Berkeley: University of California Press, www.ucpress.edu/books/pages/9518.html.

The New York Times 2004. "Groundhog day, editorial," *The New York Times,* November 20: A18.

2005. "Strange behavior at the F.D.A.," *The New York Times,* November 15: A26.

NewsHour 2003. "Rumsfeld defends pre- and post-Iraq war actions," *Online NewsHour,* July 9, www.pbs.org/newshour/updates/rumsfeld_07-09-03.html.

Nigg, Joanne M. 2000. "Predicting earthquakes: science, pseudoscience and public policy paradox," in Daniel Sarewitz, Roger A. Pielke Jr., and Radford Byerly Jr. (eds.), *Prediction: science, decision-making, and the future of nature.* Washington, DC: Island Press, pp. 135–156.

NIST Physics Laboratory 2006. "The NIST reference on constants, units, and uncertainty: uncertainty of measurement results," Physics Laboratory, http://physics.nist.gov/cuu/Uncertainty/glossary.html.

Nowotny, Helga, Scott, Peter, and Gibbons, Michael 2001. *Re-thinking science: knowledge and the public in an age of uncertainty.* Cambridge: Polity Press.

Office of Technology Assessment 1991. *Federally funded research: decisions for a decade.* Washington, DC: OTA-SET-490, US GPO.

Oreskes, Naomi 2004. "Science and public policy: what's proof got to do with it?," *Environmental Science & Policy* 7: 369–383.

Oreskes, Naomi, Shrader-Frechette, Kristin and Belitz, Kenneth. 1994. "Verification, validation, and confirmation of numerical models in the earth sciences," *Science* 263 (5147): 641–646.

Parker-Pope, Tara 2002. "Women are still urged to get mammograms despite debate," *The Wall Street Journal,* February 8.

Peat, F. David 2002. *From certainty to uncertainty: the story of science and ideas in the twentieth century.* Washington, DC: Joseph Henry Press.

Petracca, Mark P. 1992. *The politics of interests: interest groups transformed.* Boulder: Westview Press.

Pielke, Roger A., Jr. 2002. "Science policy: policy, politics and perspective," *Nature* 416: 367–368, www.nature.com/nature/journal/v416/n6879/full/416367a.html.

2004a. "Forests, tornadoes, and abortion: thinking about science, politics and policy," in Karen Arabas and Joe Bowersox (eds.), *Forest futures: science, policy and politics for the next century,* Lanham, MD: Rowman and Littlefield, pp. 143–152.

2004b. "When scientists politicize science: making sense of controversy over *The skeptical environmentalist,*" *Environmental Science & Policy* 7: 405–417.

Pielke, Roger A., Jr. 2004c. "The cherry pick," *Ogmius* 8 (May), http://sciencepolicy.colorado.edu/ogmius/archives/issue_8/intro.html.

2005. "Misdefining 'climate change': consequences for science and action," *Environmental Science & Policy* 8 (6): 548–561, http://science policy.colorado.edu/admin/publication_files/resource-1841-2004.10.pdf.

Pielke, Roger A., Jr. and Betsill, Michele M. 1997. "Policy for science for policy: ozone depletion and acid rain revisited," *Research Policy* 26: 157–168, http://sciencepolicy.colorado.edu/admin/publication_files/resource-153-1997.11.pdf.

Pielke, Roger A., Jr. and Byerly, Radford, Jr. 1998. "Beyond basic and applied," *Physics Today* 51 (2): 42–46, http://sciencepolicy.colorado.edu/admin/pub-lication_files/resource-166-1998.12.pdf.

Pielke, Roger A., Jr. and Sarewitz, Daniel 2003. "Wanted: scientific leadership on climate," *Issues in Science and Technology* (Winter): 27–30, http://sciencepolicy.colorado.edu/admin/publication_files/2003.01.pdf.

Pielke, Roger A., Jr., Landsea, Chris, Mayfield, Max, Laver, James, and Pasch, Richard 2005. "Hurricanes and global warming," *Bulletin of the American Meteorological Society* 86:1571–1575.

Pimm, Stuart 2003. "Letter to the editor: Lomborg overlooked compelling information that did not fit thesis," *Financial Times*, January 20: 20.

Polanyi, Michael 1962. "The republic of science," *Minerva* (1): 54–73.

Postel, Danny 2002. "Did the shootouts over "arming America" divert atten-tion from the real issues?," *The Chronicle of Higher Education*, February 1: A12, http://chronicle.com/free/v48/i21/21a01201.htm.

Powell, Colin L. 2003. "Remarks to the United Nations Security Council," February 5, www.state.gov/secretary/former/powell/remarks/2003/17300.htm.

Preist, Dana and Pincus, Walter 2003. "Search in Iraq finds no banned weapons," *The Washington Post*, October 3: A01.

Radio National 2002. "The skeptical environmentalist," transcript of The Science Show on Australian Radio National, Robyn Williams, Bjørn Lomborg, and Peter Raven, March 2, www.abc.net.au/rn/science/ss/stories/s495345.htm.

Rayner, Steve 2003. "Democracy in the age of assessment: reflections on the roles of expertise and democracy in public-sector decision-making," *Science and Public Policy* 30 (3): 163–170.

2004. "The international challenge of climate change: thinking beyond Kyoto," *Consortium for Science, Policy and Outcomes Perspectives*, www.cspo.org/ourlibrary/perspectives/Rayner_January05.htm.

Rayner, Steve and Malone, Elizabeth L. 1998. "Ten suggestions for policy-makers," in Steve Rayner and Elizabeth Malone L. (eds.), *Human choice and climate change, vol. 4: What have we learned*. Columbus, OH: Battelle Press, pp. 109–138.

Regalado, Antonio 2003. "Global warming skeptics are facing storm clouds," *The Wall Street Journal*, July 31, http://w3g.gkss.de/staff/storch/CR-problem/cr.wsj.pdf.

Rennie, John 2002. "Misleading math about the earth: science defends itself against *The skeptical environmentalist*," *Scientific American*, January, www.sciam.com/article.cfm?articleID=000F3D47-C6D2-1CEB-93F6809EC5880000.

Risen, James, Sanger David E., and Shanker, Thom 2003. "In sketchy data, trying to gauge Iraq threat," *The New York Times*, July 20: A1, www.refuseandresist.org/war/art.php?aid=949.

Roman, Joe and Palumbi, Stephen R. 2003. "Whales before whaling in the North Atlantic," *Science* 301: 508–510, www.stanford.edu/group/Palumbi/manuscripts/Whale2003.pdf.

Rosenberg, Nathan 1982. *Inside the black box: technology and economics*. New York: Cambridge University Press.

Sarewitz, Daniel 1996. *Frontiers of illusion: science, technology, and the politics of progress*. Philadelphia: University Temple Press.

2000. "Science and environmental policy: an excess of objectivity," in Robert Frodeman (ed.), *Earth matters: the earth sciences, philosophy, and the claims of community*. Upper Saddle River, NJ: Prentice Hall, pp. 79–98, www.cspo.org/ourlibrary/ScienceandEnvironmentalPolicy.htm.

2001. "Uncertainty in science and politics: lessons from the presidential election," Consortium for Science, Policy and Outcomes Commentary.

2004. "How science makes environmental controversies worse," *Environmental Science & Policy* 7: 385–403, www.cspo.org/ourlibrary/-documents/environ_controv.pdf.

Sarewitz, Daniel and Pielke, Roger A., Jr. 2000. "Breaking the global-warming gridlock," *The Atlantic Monthly* 286 (1): 54–64, http://-sciencepolicy.colorado.edu/admin/publication_files/resource-69-2000.18.pdf.

Sarewitz, Daniel, Pielke, Roger A., Jr., and Byerly Radford, Jr. (eds.) 2000. *Prediction: science, decision-making, and the future of nature*. Washington, DC: Island Press.

Savage, J. C. 1991. "Criticism of some forecasts of the national earthquake prediction evaluation council," *Bulletin of the Seismological Society of America* 81 (3): 862–881.

Scarne, John 1986. *Scarne's new complete guide to gambling*. New York: Simon and Schuster.

SCCST 1989. *National Global Change Research Act of 1989*. Senate Committee on Commerce, Science, and Transportation. Washington, DC: US Government Printing Office, S. Hrg. 101–132, February 22.

Schattschneider, Elmer Eric 1975. *The semisovereign people: a realist's view of democracy in America*. Hinsdale, IL: The Dryden Press.

Schlesinger, Arthur, Jr. 2003. "Eyeless in Iraq," *The New York Review of Books* 50 (16), October 23, www.nybooks.com/articles/16677.

Schmid, Randolph E. 2003. "Debate over whale populations," *The Associated Press*, July 24, www.cbsnews.com/stories/2003/07/24/tech/main564976.shtml.

Schmitt, Eric 2003. "Wolfowitz stands fast amid the antiwarriors," *The New York Times* September 22: A8, http://select.nytimes.com/gst/abstract.html?res=F40F17FB355E0C718EDDA00894DB404482.

Schneider, Stephen 2002. "Global warming: neglecting the complexities," *Scientific American*, January: 62–65, www.sciam.com/article.cfm? articleID =000F3D47-C6D2-1CEB-93F6809EC5880000.

Schultz, Kathryn 2001. "Let us not praise infamous men," *Grist Magazine*, December 12, www.gristmagazine.com/books/schulz121201.asp.

Science 1883. "The future of American science," *Science* 1 (1): 1–3, www.sciencemag.org/content/volns-1/issue1/index.dtl.

Scientists and Engineers for Change 2004. "48 Nobel laureates endorse John Kerry: an open letter to the American people," June 21, www.scientistsandengineersforchange.org/nobelletter.php.

Sieh, Kerry, Stuiver, Minze, and Brillinger, David 1989. "A more precise chronology of earthquakes produced by the San Andreas fault in southern California," *Journal of Geophysical Research* 94: 603–624.

Simberloff, David 2002. "Skewed skepticism," *American Scientist*, March–April, www.americanscientist.org/template/BookReviewTypeDetail/assetid/17791.

Simon, Julian Lincoln 1996. *The ultimate resource 2*. Princeton, NJ: Princeton University Press, www.juliansimon.com/writings/Ultimate_Resource/.

Skidelsky, Robert 2000. "Skidelsky on Keynes," *The Economist*, November 25: 83–85.

Starobin, Paul 2006. "Who turned out the enlightenment," *National Journal*, July 20–26.

Stewart, Thomas R. 2000. "Uncertainty, judgment and error in prediction," in Daniel Sarewitz, Roger A. Pielke Jr., and Radford Byerly Jr., (eds.), *Prediction: science, decision-making, and the future of nature*. Washington, DC: Island Press, pp. 41–60.

Stokes, Donald E. 1995. "Sigma XI," in Kate Miller (ed.), *Vannevar Bush II: science for the 21st century*. Research Triangle Park, NC: Sigma Xi, Scientific Research Society.

Stokes, Donald E. 1997. *Pasteur's quadrant: basic science and technological innovation*. Washington, DC: Brookings Institution Press.

Strauss, Lewis L. 1954. "Speech to the National Association of Science Writers," *The New York Times*, September 17.

Union of Concerned Scientists 2003. "UCS examines *The skeptical environmentalist* by Bjørn Lomborg," Union of Concerned Scientists, www.ucsusa.org/global_environment/archive/page.cfm?pageID=533.

United Nations Charter 2006. "Chapter VII: action with respect to threats to the peace, breaches of the peace, and acts of aggression," in *Charter of the United Nations*, www.un.org/aboutun/charter/chapter7.htm.

US Department of Defense 2001. *Department of Defense dictionary of military and associated terms*. Joint Publication 1–02, April 12 (as amended through April 14, 2006). Washington, DC: US Government Printing Office, www.dtic.mil/doctrine/jel/new_pubs/jp1_02.pdf.

US Department of State 1950. "NSC 68: United States objectives and programs for national security," in *Foreign relations of the United States 1950, Volume I*, www.mtholyoke.edu/acad/intrel/nsc-68/nsc68-1.htm.

US House of Representatives Committee on Government Reform 2003. "Politics and science in the Bush administration," Minority Staff, Special Investigations Division, Politics and Science, August; updated November 13, www.house.gov/reform/min/politicsandscience/pdfs/pdf_politics_and_science_rep.pdf.

US House of Representatives Committee on Science 1998. *Unlocking our future: towards a new national science policy*. Washington, DC: Government Printing Office, Committee Print 105-B, www.access.gpo.gov/congress/house/science/cp105-b/toc.html.

US Newswire 2004a. "Kerry remarks in Denver, Colorado," *US Newswire*, June 21, http://releases.usnewswire.com/GetRelease.asp?id=32237.

2004b. "Kerry: we must lift the barriers that stand in the way of science," *US Newswire*, June 12, http://releases.usnewswire.com/GetRelease.asp?id=31802.

USDA National Agricultural Library 2006. "Dietary guidance: USDA food guide pyramid," www.nal.usda.gov/fnic/Fpyr/pyramid.html.

VegSource 2006a. "Vegetarian food pyramid," Nutritional Information, www.vegsource.com/nutrition/pyramid.htm.

2006b. "Vegan food pyramid," Nutritional Information, www.vegsource.com/nutrition/pyramid_vegan.htm.

Weinberg, Alvin Martin 1970. "The axiology of science," *American Scientist* 58: 612–617.

1992. *Nuclear reactions: science and trans-science*. New York: AIP Press.

Weingart, Peter 1999. "Scientific expertise and political accountability: paradoxes of science in politics," *Science and Public Policy* 26 (3): 151–161.

Weisman, Steven R. 2003. "Pre-emption: idea with a lineage whose time has come," *The New York Times*, March 23, www.mtholyoke.edu/acad/intrel/bush/preempt.htm.

Weiss, R. 2006. "Senators denounce scientists' stem cell claims," *Washington post*, September 7: A04.

White, Lynn, Jr. 1967. "The historical roots of our ecologic crisis," *Science* 155: 103–1207, www.bemidjistate.edu/peoplenv/lynnwhite.htm.

White House 2001a. "President discusses stem cell research," August 9, www.whitehouse.gov/news/releases/2001/08/20010809-2.html.

2001b. "President Bush discusses global climate change," June 11, www.whitehouse.gov/news/releases/2001/06/20010611-2.html.

2002. "The national security strategy of the United States of America," September 17. Washington, DC, www.whitehouse.gov/nsc/ nss.pdf.

Wise, George 1985. "Science and technology," *Osiris*, 2nd series, Historical Writing on American Science (1): 229–246.

Woodard, Colin 2001. "The tabloid environmentalist: how a pseudo-scientist duped the big media – big time," TomPaine.com, December 7, www.tompaine.com/Archive/scontent/4747.html.

World Bank Group 2003. "The World Bank/WWF forest alliance," World Bank/WWF Alliance for Forest Conservation and Sustainable Use, http://lnweb18.worldbank.org/essd/envext.nsf/80ParentDoc/WBWWFForestAlliance?Opendocument.

World Resources Institute 2001. "Media kit: debunking pseudo-scholarship: things a journalist should know about *The Skeptical Environmentalist*," World Resources Institute, November 9, http://newsroom.wri.org/mediakits_contents.cfm?MediaKitID=1.

Wright, Karen 2000. "Works in progress: even the best technology in the world can't seem to calculate how high this mountain really is," *Discover* 21 (5), www.discover.com/issues/may-00/departments/featworks/.

Wunsch, Carl 1999. "The interpretation of short climate records, with comments on the north Atlantic and southern oscillations," *Bulletin of the American Meteorological Society* 80 (2): 245–256, ams.allenpress. com/ pdfserv/10.1175/1520-0477(1999)080<0245: TIOSCR>2.0.CO;2.

Wynne, Brian 1991. "Knowledges in context," *Science, Technology & Human Values* 16 (1): 111–121.

Wynne, Brian, Wilsdon, James, and Stilgoe, Jack 2005. *The public value of science*. London: Demos.

Index

Numbers in italics indicate a reference to a table or figure